What The Heck Is Prayer Anyway?

Tracey McReynolds

"What The Heck Is Prayer Anyway"

Foreward

"What The Heck Is Prayer Anyway?" by Tracey McReynolds is an excellent must-read book that speaks to the deepest cry of the heart and soul to make contact with Jesus – and encounter Him.

If you have a personal relationship with Jesus – yet desire a deeper, tangible, intimate relationship with Jesus – then you need to get this book and read it! Believe me, it is an amazing journey of one godly lady who has such a deep desire and passion for more of Jesus by which He revealed Himself to her in many remarkable ways. She seems ordinary like everyone one else… until the Holy Spirit moves on her in extraordinary ways. As a minister of the gospel, I have witnessed _and_ experienced many unusual things in the heavenly realm, yet this book opened my eyes to envision even "deeper things" and how God uses ordinary people like Tracey to accomplish kingdom business through worship and intercessory prayer. It is said we pray out mysteries when we pray in the spirit, and Tracey's story is a marvelous testimony of how God can use anyone to advance His kingdom through prayer. Layer by layer, Tracey takes us on her 20-year intercessory journey to tell us what she thinks and ponders as the Lord takes her "deep unto deep" – and then she reveals how the Holy Spirit is able to operate in us and through us once we yield to His prompting and anointing – whereby the ordinary becomes extraordinary. If you want to experience extraordinary, then get this book, read it – and get ready for "WOW… that's amazing!"

When believers operate as intercessors, we may not know to what extent our prayers have on other people or nations, but I can assure you – you are shifting atmospheres in your community that causes the gates of Hell to shake. During one of Tracey's prayer events, she was shifting human history half way around the world. So I ask you, do you want to be known as a world changer? When you get to the other side, how do you want to be remembered? As someone who was just a good person… or as someone who walked in the power and anointing of the Spirit that caused demons to tremble? That, my friend, can be _your_ eternal identity in Christ – because that is what you were called to do by faith – because Jesus gave you authority over devils and demons through prayer! If you are involved in prayer ministry as a prayer warrior, an intercessor or a prophetic intercessor, then this book will bless you. Your desire to wait in stillness for long periods of time to encounter Jesus and be used by Him – will also be blessed and rewarded by Him.

I know Tracey personally and I encourage you to read her testimony! Her message is simple: seek Jesus – love Jesus – and get ready for your own divine encounter! You'll learn how greater things are accomplished through prayer… whereby you are able to shift the world around you from darkness to light.

Go now, therefore… and be a bright light (Matt. 5:14)! Your world will never be the same… and (after all) isn't that the main point of "Christ in you"?

- Paul Tubach, Jr.
Author of the Image Bearer Series
Imaginist and Revivalist at Newearthministries.org

Dedication

To my mother who has passed on to glory. She is the reason I'm serving Jesus today. I will never forget how she pursued God with her whole heart. She was truly my example of what it means to go after God. I know she would be so proud. I love and miss you Mom!

Book Endorsements

"What the heck is prayer anyway?" captured me from the start! It portrays the yearnings of the heart for a greater reality-and the vulnerability of the heart to not stay in the yearning but be captivated by the willingness.

The Author was raised in a Christian home, she knew of Him but truly desired the unknown, what she had heard of but never experienced personally. She unfolds the ability to be still, step out of the comfort zone and into the fullness of His glory. It's a captivating story, her life was transformed where most of us stand in the fear of the unknown. This book will captivate your purpose for His kingdom here on earth the "worth" of facing the fear of the unknown. Her story inspired me to step out of the yearning and into the uncomfortable, left me wanting more of the Holy Spirit, more than just the everyday here I am God . This story touches the heart and gives hope to those struggling with the "I know you have more God " what does it look like? How do I get it? Is there someone out there that feels the way I do?

The unknown becomes the known.

- April Parrish, PRS
Woman's Home Director – Regenesis

I met Tracey 34 years ago as we sat in class together at Rhema Bible Training Center. She was 18 and fresh out of High School, and we have remained friends all these years. Every time we would see each other, we would discuss our journey in God, marriage, raising kids, and life in general. This story, however, is the story about a radical shift in her life that began in 2002 when she encountered the God of the universe on a whole other level. You will discover in detail how spiritual hunger and obedience can transform you (as it did her) from an average Christian into a person who can have numerous personal and intimate encounters with God.

I believe, as you read these pages and see Tracey's transparency and desire for God, her journey will challenge you to seek God and believe you can also achieve intimacy with Him. It's possible for your life to be radically changed through real encounters with God, and these supernatural encounters can radically change your world as well.

Tracey's personal quest to know more of God resulted in many supernatural experiences during worship and prayer that left her questioning much of what was happening to her. In her search for answers, she explains how heaven came and kissed her as she worshiped and how she discovered deeper places in the Glory of God. These pages will challenge you to embark on your own journey to find the Creator of Heaven and Earth to experience a personal one-on-one encounter with God in all His Glory.

Mathew 5:6 "Blessed are they which
do **hunger and thirst** after righteousness: for they
shall be filled."
John 6:35 "And Jesus said unto them, I am the
bread of life: he that cometh to Me shall
never **hunger**; and he that believeth on Me shall
never thirst."

Evangelist Ronda Moore
Voice Of Revival Ministries International
Tampa, Fl.
Carrying Revival to The Nations of The World

"What the Heck is Prayer Anyway?" is an account
of Tracey's journey into the deep places of
God. Whether you have been there before or this is
your first journey; the honest, raw surrender that
leaps off the pages of this book will stir within you
the cry for more and draw you into the
understanding of the limitless possibilities in God!

- Pastor Jenny West

As Leonard Ravenhill said, "A man with an
experience GOD is never at the mercy of a man with
an argument." Tracey has lived out this truth as her
powerful experiences with The Triune God over
these many years testify. Her testimony opens
hearts to the MORE of God and it's transforming
power in prayer.

- Nancy Helring, Intercessor

I have known Tracey for over 38 years as she was the daughter of a dear friend of mine. We reconnected when her mom was going through treatment for cancer and Tracey came home to be with her during that difficult season. We shared many intimate times of worship and prayer during those months, and ever since. Tracey is uncompromised and passionate about her faith in God and her love of the Word. That comes through as she shares her story of seeking Jesus with her whole heart, soul, mind and spirit. You will be encouraged as she shares her story of uncompromising faith and joy.

Deuteronomy 6:5
You shall love the Lord your God with all your heart and with all your soul and with all your might.

-Cheryl Sikorski, Intercessor

What a great read. Have you ever struggled to maintain that "first love" relationship with the Lord? It seems that everybody has the answer and is quick to share it. You've heard it, we just need to read the Bible more, pray more, and go to church more, all good things. If you want to hear how an encounter with God can make a permanent change, this is a must read. Bring tissues.

- Don Wilson- Elder SLWC

Tracey Is a woman of God, an anointed Psalmist, and a trusted friend. We are fellow Colleagues in the trenches together. I love her and I love what the Lord has done in her life and is continuing to do. I recommend her new ground breaking book and I pray it will put a spark in you to have your own personal revival with the Lord.

-Kim Osborn, Co-Leader and Prophetic Psalmist with New Harvest Ministries International

A GOOD READ for sure. For me, the resounding theme of the book was centered on the power of an "encounter." It was compelling to see a "Plain Jane" become transformed not only by receiving Christ but also by her strong desire to dive deeper into the mysteries of God through the Power of the Holy Spirit. I was fascinated by the events that led up to and followed the "encounter" and could truly relate to the various startling reactions to the manifestations of the Holy Spirit, especially from people of faith.

Ultimately I believe this book will help those that
have had a true "encounter" see that... they are not
alone.

- Marcus Walker. CPRS
Program Director
Regenesis

God is real and this book gives evidence of that! I
believe that by reading, you will be touched and gain
a better understanding of His power.

- Kenny Snyder
Lover of Jesus

Table of Contents

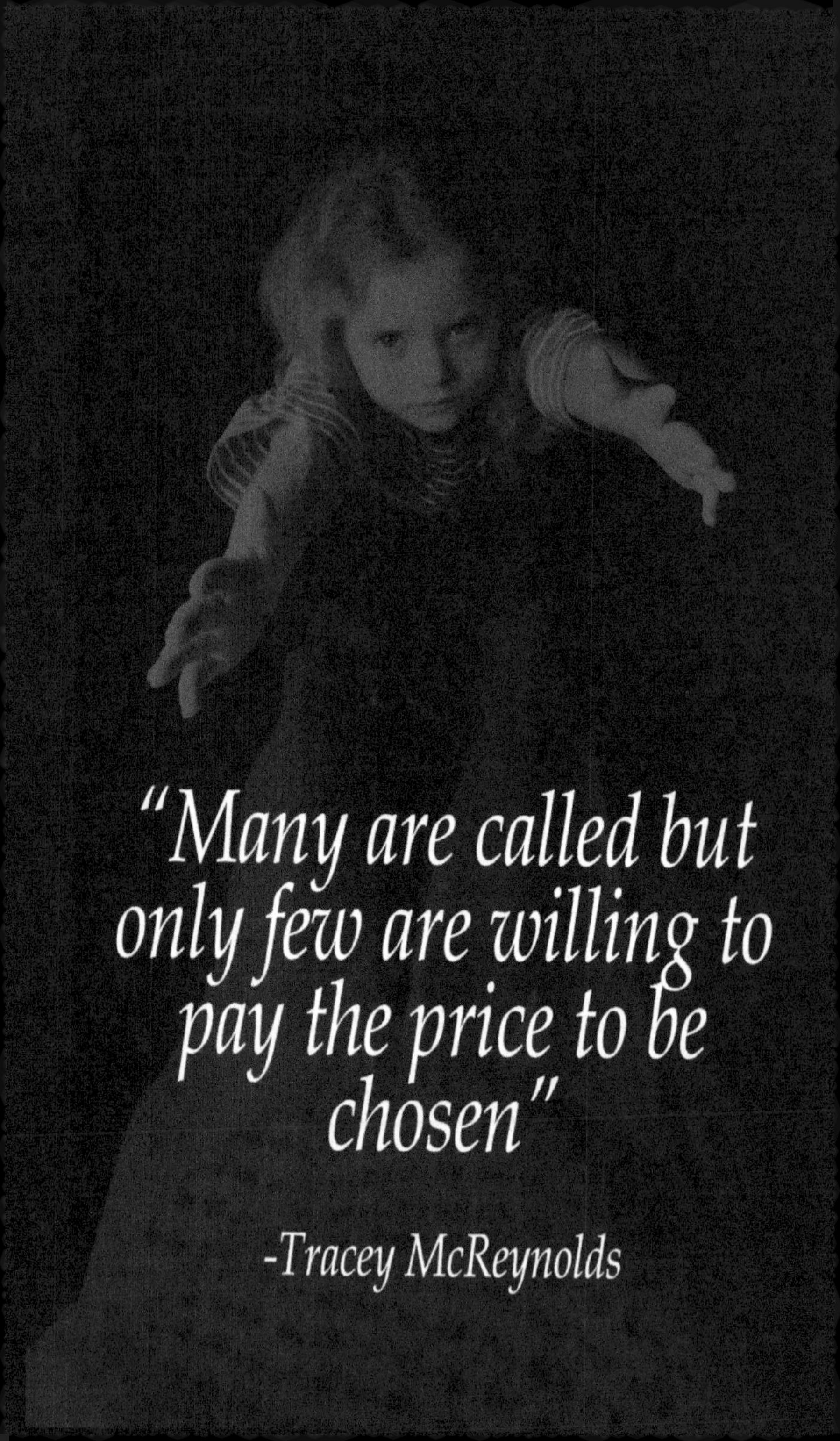

"Many are called but only few are willing to pay the price to be chosen"

-Tracey McReynolds

What The Heck Is Prayer Anyway

Introduction

I love stories, I love reading stories and I love
hearing people share their stories; everybody has a
story, and this is my story.   My story is not one of
trauma or abuse or a battle with an addiction; it is a
story of my pursuit to follow Christ.   It's a story of
obedience, the story of dying to self, laying down my
dreams, and my desire to follow after Him.

Our world needs an encounter with the Most High
God. Christians need an encounter. And how do I
know? Because I needed an encounter! I may not
have even known I needed one, but God knew I
needed one more than I knew I needed one. I
heard a preacher say, "You can never crave what
you have never tasted." The world is searching for
Love. They are searching for answers. They are
searching for purpose. The world most likely doesn't
even know that it needs an encounter with God.

Before my encounter with God, my walk as a
Christian was very average like many of you. Most
of the time, I really didn't even want to go to church;
my parents and husband had to drag me. I was a
young married soldier in the United States Army and
I was raising two young kids. I went to Bible school
because I did really love God and I knew I was not
college material. I am definitely more "brawn" than

"brain".   While I was in Bible school, I was more infatuated with my soon to be husband more than I was God, but I was only 19 at the time. All in all, I was a pretty average nominal once a week Sunday church Christian.

To some, this book may be offensive. Many will say this is not God. God is not that way. How do I know this? Because this is what I have already been told by some Christians. That is religion talking – when He doesn't fit into our mold of the God that we think we know yet can't explain – we get offended. Who does anyone think they are to say God will only do this or only move this way? God can do whatever He wants; however, He wants whomsoever He wants. I heard a minister say, "God moves through many signs and miracles that make you wonder."

✦

Romans 15:19 "Through mighty signs and wonders, by the power of the Spirit of God; so that from Jerusalem, and round about unto Illyricum, I have fully preached the gospel of Christ."

✦

I pray as you read my story that it will stir your faith and you will be inspired to pursue Him harder with all your heart. My prayer is that the anointing of the Holy Spirit rests on the pages of this book and you are blessed by reading this.

What happen to me is sovereign and undeniable.

My prayer is you have an encounter with God as well.

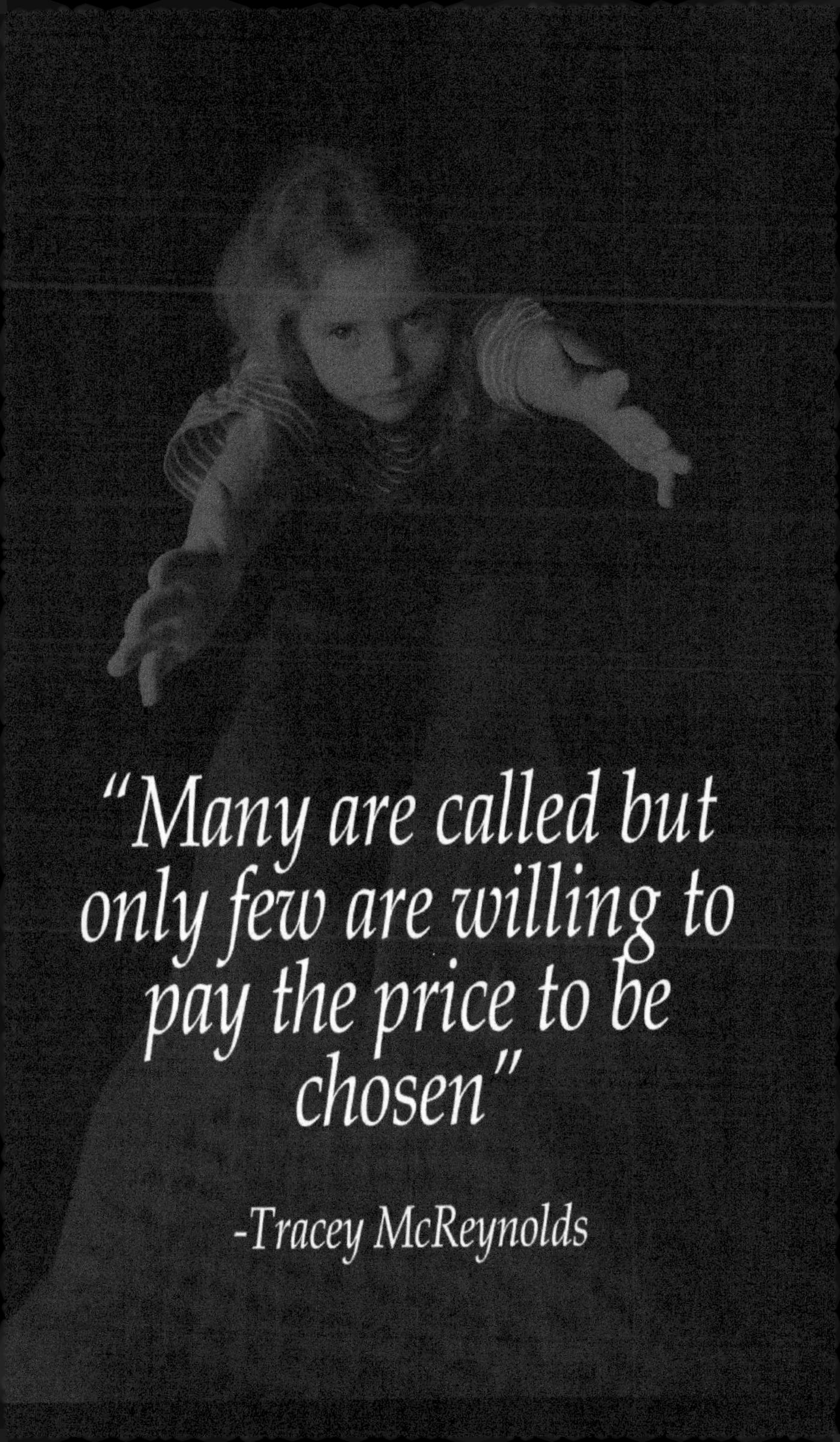

"Many are called but only few are willing to pay the price to be chosen"

-Tracey McReynolds

Chapter 1
My Beginning

I grew up in a good Christian home; I did not drink or smoke, but I did try cigarettes (once). My schoolmate's mom smoked "More" cigarettes (those skinny long brown ones). We stole six out of her mom's purse and smoked them down by the railroad tracks while looking for rocks for our six-grade science project. That is the only time I ever smoked cigarettes and to this day I disdain them. I did have one Bailey's Irish Cream alcoholic drink on New Year's Eve back when I was in high school, but I never liked alcohol and I hate beer! I had a summer job and one of my friends and I cleaned the bathrooms at a marina in downtown Hudson, Wisconsin where I grew up. People would leave their old nasty smelly discarded beer cans with cigarette butts shoved in them and I was the one that had to clean up after them. So, to this day, because I had that experience, I have no desire to drink beer or smoke. The only man I have ever been with is my husband (who I meet in Bible school). My husband is a Godly man and I am his one and only. The only time I have been drunk is "in the Spirit" and only time I've been high is at the dentist on the laughing gas when I got my wisdom teeth pulled. I did skinny dip a time or two, in the St. Croix River in Hudson, Wisconsin. That is pretty much the extent of my carnal sinful past. But, yes, as I have grown and gotten older, God is – and will continually be – dealing with the sins of my heart. That's the place where it really matters! After all, the Bible does say the issues of life flow out of the heart. Overall, God did bless me with a good upbringing, and I am very thankful. Moving on...

My Mother led me to Christ when I was around 13 years old, though not in a very good way I might add. I remember that day well. We lived at 803 7th Street, in Hudson, Wisconsin. It was a rainy day. I was in the living room sitting on our white couch with a blue and green paisley print while staring out the large bay window watching the rain. Mom decided she was going to tell me about the rapture. She told me all about the rapture and how she was saved and all the people who were saved would be caught up with Jesus and that when Jesus came – if I wasn't saved – she would be taken up in the clouds and I would be all alone. Basically, Jesus was going to take my Mommy, so of course I got scared and prayed the sinner's prayer and got saved. I mean, bless her heart, but that is not how you should lead someone to Christ. I, however, about a year or so later did make my public profession of faith at Speak The Word Church in uptown Minneapolis, MN during a Roberts Liardon meeting (when he was 16 or 17 years old at the time). He was speaking about an encounter he had in Heaven as a little boy when he was just 8 years old. I was thinking how bold and powerful this teenage boy was preaching about God and I was completely intrigued and drawn to his testimony. With butterflies in my stomach and my heart pounding, I went forward in that old church (with wooden pews covered with red cushions, dark wooden ornate carpentry, red carpet) and walked down the center isle and accepted Jesus Christ as my Lord and Savior. I was then taken to another room and received the Baptism of the Holy Spirit and spoke in tongues. I didn't speak in tongues right away; I was coached and did the whole repeat the tongue after me (to like "prime the pump"). I did eventually speak and the tongues flowed. I can't imagine not having the Baptism of the Holy Spirit and not speaking in tongues. I have spoken in my prayer language for 38 years! I don't remember the exact date I got saved, but I remember where I was, the church building, and the service where I got saved. It is still a vivid memory (and quite the opposite experience that I had with my mother).

Serving Christ is not easy – especially when he asks you to give up things that your flesh does not want you to give up. But, oh… it's so worth it. Some things that I will be sharing later on in this book… people may be skeptical about and not believe it, but I love this statement: "a man with an experience is never at the mercy of a man with an argument."

You cannot explain an infinite God with a finite mind. Understand this - it's by faith! When the encounters and experiences were happening to me, I was judged and condemned quite strongly by Bible believing, Spirit-filled, Charismatic Christians, but I wouldn't trade any of it for the encounters and experiences that I had with God. I would go through the persecution and judgment again, and take the ridicule for what I learned, experienced, and how I encountered Him – because I am and will never be the same. I will provide as much scripture as possible to back up what happened to me.

A scripture in the Bible says, "Many are called, but few are chosen" Matthew 22:14 (KJV). I like to say: many are called, but only few are willing to pay the price to be chosen. I believe that God gave me opportunities of radical obedience to prove to Him that I was serious about going after Him and pursuing Him. God will not ask you for things you <u>are</u> willing to give up, but rather – he will ask you for those things that you're <u>not</u> willing to give up, such as the things that you hold near and dear, the things that are close to your heart, the things that you have put your hope in, your faith in, your trust in, and your confidence in. Really, those are the things that are taking His place in your life… and those are the exact things He will ask for. What you cannot walk away from becomes your master. You will see how much things have a grip on you… when you're asked to let them go.

My mother always encouraged me in my Christian walk with the Lord. She would always call me up and ask me "did you pray in tongues today?" "Have you read your Bible?" She would always buy me prayer journals and books about walking in the Christian faith. She would buy my kids Christian videos, books, and one year she gave both of them a shofar (or what some call a ram's horn) for Christmas. She was a lover of God for sure.

My mom, Jan Anderson, is the reason I am serving Jesus today. My mother had a rough upbringing. My grandfather was an alcoholic and my grandmother was a cold, unaffectionate, strict lady. I heard stories that grandma would lock my aunt in the closet for hours; not sure why; never heard the whole story. Mom named me after her grandmother, Tracy. She got her love and affection from her, and she adored her grandma, Tracy Kessler. I don't remember her story of when she got saved, but as long as I can remember… mom sought God. He was her saving grace – and – her sanctuary during her difficult upbringing. We went to a Lutheran Church growing up and we never heard sermons about being "born again" that I can remember. She was hungry for more of God. She knew there was more in God. She heard about the Holy Spirit and received the baptism of the Holy Spirit, then we left the Lutheran Church and started attending Speak The Word Church in Minneapolis, MN, where I got saved. We would drive an hour to that church because, as they would say, "A Church that's alive is worth the drive." Mom was always, always seeking out new ministries and preachers who had a fresh revelation and a "Now" word of the Lord.

My parents divorced after 26 years of marriage. I was 19 at the time. It was tough, but mom never stopped seeking God. My mom passed at the age of 61 from ovarian cancer when I was only 34. I believe she died not from the cancer but from a broken heart. She always struggled to forgive my grandma for her upbringing, she dealt with going through divorce, and she had a strained relationship with my brother. I questioned the Lord about my mom's death. She did everything right, she prayed, went to healing services, and totally changed her diet. I heard a preacher say "the body can't heal when it's in pain." God is so faithful; that's how I got my answer about mom. Mom had so much emotional pain in her heart; her body was never at rest, and with all that stress… her body couldn't heal. He is sovereign and I trust Him. It's hard, but I still trust Him. She's been gone 17 years now and, of course, it goes without saying: I miss her. You may wonder why I'm sharing about my family; I'm bringing it up to show you how average I am and how (to a certain degree) all of our lives are filled with a little bit of dysfunction, including mine, but that doesn't matter to God necessarily. You don't have to be perfect to be used by God, which none of us will ever be anyway. Only God is perfect.

Kathryn Kuhlman used to say, "God is not looking for golden vessels or silver vessels, just available vessels, because they are the rarest." Even with my dysfunction, He saw that I was available with a heart towards Him and He chose me.

I distinctly remember one day (after I got off the phone with my mom) saying to the Lord, "Prayer, what the heck really is prayer anyway?" I honestly believe that was the day God decided He was going to show me what prayer was and He was going to reveal himself to me because I had a hunger in my heart for Him (but I just really didn't know how to go after Him or pursue Him). Well, He certainly heard me when I asked that question… and that is what this book is about!

I mean, I knew that prayer was talking to God, but prayer is so much more: going deeper; getting closer; deeper intimacy. I wasn't really sure about how to go about it, and I wasn't around anyone (or knew of anyone) who was into seeking God like that. Yes, I went to Bible school, but there weren't any classes taught on intimacy with God (that I recall). So, that is what I meant when I said, "What the heck is prayer anyway?"

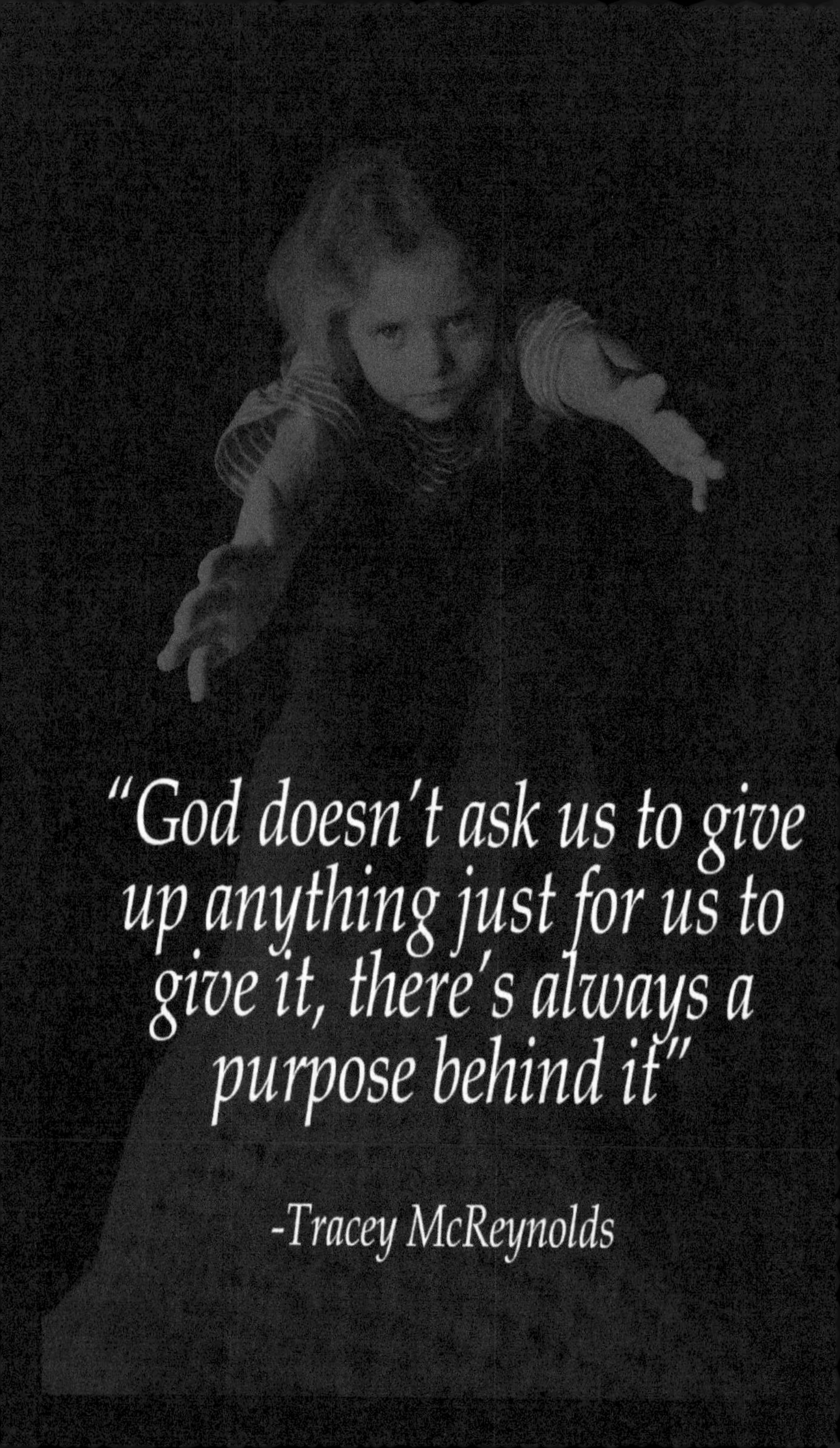

"God doesn't ask us to give up anything just for us to give it, there's always a purpose behind it"

-Tracey McReynolds

Chapter 2
Beginning of the Testing

✦

John 12:24 "Verily, verily, I say unto you, except a corn of wheat fall into the ground and die, it abideth alone: but if it die, it bringeth forth much fruit." (KJV)

✦

Before my radical encounter with God on January 20, 2002, there were three very large tests and acts of obedience that God required of me. I believe these tests of obedience were tests God presented to me – to be chosen by Him. I love this scripture in Psalms:

✦

Psalms 65:4 "Blessed is the man You choose, and cause to approach You, that he may dwell in Your courts. We shall be satisfied with the goodness of

✦

These acts of obedience and tests were kind of intermingled, but happened over the course of a few years, because I was stubborn and bullheaded and did not want to surrender. God must have seen something in my heart, though, because He just kept pressing me and pressing me. The Holy Spirit is sometimes called the "Holy Hound of Heaven" and he will hound you and hound you until you finally surrender. He remembers prayers and vows of surrender that we say to Him in times of worship and also prayers that we may have even forgotten.

✦

Numbers 30:2 "If a man makes a vow to the LORD, or swears an oath to bind himself by some agreement, he shall not break his word; he shall do according to all that proceeds out of his mouth." *(NKJV)*

✦

Everything that God asks us to give up – we think it's a loss. We are not losing anything, but we are gaining what He has for us because… when we let go of what's in our hand… He can let go of what is in His hand… and He certainly has the bigger hand.

✦

Mark 8:36 "For what shall it profit a man, if he shall gain the whole world, and lose his own soul?" (KJV)

✦

Everything God tested and challenged me – were about things near and dear to me; my home, my finances and my singing. Testing is not easy at the time. Let me rephrase that: testing is never easy. Thinking back to those times, though – it was tough; they were my Isaac's, but oh so worth it all.

After I asked the Lord "what the heck really is prayer anyways?" I had some extremely tormenting thoughts of death. I believe the enemy was observing these acts of sacrifice and obedience and he knows (throughout history) that God always rewards people who yield to Him. The enemy (or Satan) probably figured I was on the cusp of a spiritual breakthrough, so he attempted to put fear in me. I began having tormenting thoughts of death and these thoughts were continuous. I heard "you're gonna die, you're gonna die" when I woke up, and I heard it pretty much all day. These thoughts lasted nearly a month. I had never experienced this type of torment. Not only was it tormenting me, it was harassing me as well, so much so, that I would put my hands on my head to try and quiet those thoughts, and cover my face and act like I was trying to shield myself (as if it was external and physical even though it was internal and spiritual and, of course, that did nothing). It did put fear in me – and it was awful! I prayed and stood against it and then it finally lifted. It was indeed an intense time of spiritual warfare. Sometime after this month or so, the testing began and I entered "HSU" Holy Spirit University, where you never fail any tests; you just keep taking them over and over until you pass!

My Tests

Test #1 – My Beloved House

We live in Central Virginia and I wanted to have a classic Virginian home. I wanted a colonial style brick home with columns, large trim, old wavy windows… a Circa 1920's classic good ole' Virginian home. We had lived in a modern home because that was the first house we got when we came to Virginia. We were told the house we lived in actually before we bought it was a "Frank Lloyd Wright" style design, farthest thing from colonial, but I kept telling Gary that I wanted a colonial home, so we continued flipping and remodeling houses while we sought to find a colonial that we could work on and eventually move in.

Let me pause and take a minute and talk about my wonderful Husband, Gary. We met at Rhema Bible Training Center (Kenneth Hagins Bible School). It was located in Broken Arrow, Oklahoma, a suburb of Tulsa. Rhema was sometimes called, "Rhema Bridal Training Center, where you got your ring by Spring." Well, we've been married for 32 years; he has been with me every step of the way and has always encouraged me and supported me in my walk with God. He would joke and say God always talked to me about surrendering and being tested (with giving or surrendering things) because he, Gary, is already a giver and it's easy for him to let go. If I let him, Gary would give everything we own away. He used to tell me that he would live in a trailer and eat beans and rice if God told him too. I would always get so mad when he would say that! My mom would always say, Gary has such a "poverty spirit." I know now what she meant. Gary was willing to surrender all to Jesus if He asked him too. He has always been this way. Everything he does is with God's Kingdom in mind. He actually grew up attending Kathryn Kuhlman's Church, in Youngstown, Ohio, in the Stambaugh Auditorium. He got saved in her 2nd grade Sunday School Class, when he was around 7 years old. His family attended there until he was 12 years old so he saw the powerful demonstration of the Holy Spirit even at a young age. One thing is… is he has remained constant and stable in my life with all the (seemingly) craziness going on with me. He accepts it. He is a lover of God. He will defend the Gospel of Jesus Christ and fight for the Kingdom of God. He preaches righteousness and holiness and right living before men and God. He has corrected me many a time when I was not acting Christ-like, and I will mention more about Gary later on.

Well, we found this great Dutch colonial with clapboard siding on a quiet dead end street. Needless to say, it was quite a sight. An older couple with four kids and two rescued Great Dane dogs (that peed all over the house, yuck) owned the house.   The decor was stuck in the 1970s, it had acoustic drop office ceilings to hide the broken plaster and dark wood paneling throughout the entire home, orange shag carpet, a red velvet paisley wallpapered entry, greasy gross kitchen pine cabinets and at least 20 years of overgrowth outside. The place was filthy, to say the least. We saw all the "good bones"; it had all the trim and all the classic colonial features, so we went ahead and got a loan and started working on it. Gary is quite a talented handyman, so we pretty much did all the work ourselves. We stripped off all the paneling, removed the acoustic tile drop ceilings, put in all new sheet rock, painted the entire house (inside and out), had the hardwood floors refinished, installed a new kitchen with white kitchen cabinets, completely remodeled the bathrooms, added new light fixtures, and re-landscaped.   We even turned the side porch into a sunroom with some large windows we got for free from a neighbor who did some upgrades and replaced their windows. We gave this house a lot of time and personal attention due to the fact that we were a struggling young family (living sacrificially), and all the work and repairs became sentimental. I loved this house so much! I took all the brass doorknobs and plates off every door and stripped the paint off them and shined them with Brasso. I even stripped the paint off the hinges. Did I say that I loved this house? I mean… I really loved this house! I can remember standing in my bathroom window during one fall day looking through the wavy leaded glass windows at our neighbors' two large maple trees with bright yellow leaves on bright sunny days and just being completely content; it was so beautiful. We had planned to stay and I made up my mind I was never going to move, but God had another plan.

God started impressing on me that we needed to put our house up for sale, and I remember going out for walks and God would be telling me that we needed to sell the house. Seriously God??? My walks were also my prayer time and very precious and always enjoyable to me… until he started talking to me about giving up the house. I literally put my hand up in the air (behind me) and said to God, "I'm not listening to you God, I am not listening, don't talk to me" and I said to the Lord one time, "talk to the hand" (I can't believe I actually did that thinking back now). That shows you just how much I made this house that I loved… more important than obeying God. Like I said, the Holy Spirit can sometimes be called "The Holy hound of Heaven." He doesn't change His mind and He kept pressing on me and pressing on me to sell our house. I think it took me six months to a year to finally obey. I'm not sure, but at the time… the real estate sales market was horrible in our area and nothing was selling. It was taking houses at least six months to sell and of course I'm thinking this (while He is telling me to sell the house). I finally decided, "Alright, Lord, I'm going to obey you". I was obedient, but not very willing. So we put out a For Sale By Owner Sign (FSBO) fleece in the front yard on a Sunday afternoon. I was not expecting anything. We went to church that evening and came home and had a voicemail on our answering machine with someone interested in our home. I could not believe it. I mean it hadn't even been 24 hours since we put the sign out in the front yard. The couple came and saw the house and put an offer on it, but they were unable to get a bank loan, but two weeks later another couple came and ended up buying the house. Again, I could not believe it; in a depressed real estate market, we actually sold our house. God already knew it was going to sell fast. It was no surprise to Him.

While we are in the process of selling our house, Gary was asked by our local church to go over to Liberia, Africa, to be the lay minister there while the head missionary was taking care of personal business back in the United States. And because we had sold our beloved house, the kids and I had money to live on while Gary was gone for two months so he could do the Lord's work.

Also, during that time, we had turned our first home (the Mid-century modern one) into a discounted rental home for the new associate pastor and his family at our church. When we sold our Dutch Colonial, the timing worked out perfect and we were able to move back into that house as the Pastor and his family moved into their newly purchased home. So, we moved back into our first house and did some upgrades and lived there a few more years.

A couple years later (after we sold the house and after everything that happened with me by the Holy Spirit), I would drive by my old Dutch Colonial house and look at it with shame, and think… I cannot believe I actually told God "talk to the hand" and say I was not moving. What was I was thinking? I was choosing this house that is temporal and going to "burn" over listening to the voice of the Lord. Still to this day I drive by it and I think to myself, "I'm so glad I chose you God and I'm sorry, for how I behaved." Again, what was I thinking?

As a continuation of the housing story, we ended up living in a bigger house on the same street but on the best part of the street with two acres of beautiful gardens. This house was so nice that the house and gardens were featured on our city's annual spring garden tour. Why do we doubt God? He always has good things in store for us, better than the stuff we are trying to hold onto.

I cannot say that I am quicker, now, to obey the Lord. Case in point: He told me two years ago to share my testimony and write this book, yet I have been arguing with Him. Sometimes I obey faster than other times, but I definitely need to obey quicker. Delayed obedience is called: disobedience!

I Samuel 15:22 "And Samuel said, Hath the Lord as great delight in burnt offerings and sacrifices, as in obeying the voice of the Lord? Behold, to obey is better than sacrifice, and to hearken than the fat of rams." (KJV)

Test #2 – Giving half a year income

The church we were attending was in a building program and raising money to build a new building, and our Bishop came to our church to preach one

Sunday. I remember he was ministering a sermon about "vows that we had made to God" for this or that, and about giving us the opportunity to make amends with the Lord for not completing the vow. At the end of the service, he asked individuals to come forward for prayer and I felt that I had not lived up to my Christian commitment to the Lord on certain things, so I decided to go to the altar for prayer. While I was standing up at the altar, I heard the Lord say: "give all the money from the sale of the house we were flipping to the church" I about fell over and could not believe what I heard. I began to doubt and I questioned myself, was this me? Or could have been Satan putting these thoughts in my mind? I felt it was the Lord, but it seems to me to be a mind blowing request!

The house we had remodeled and were flipping was just two doors down from "the modern" house we lived in. Up to this point we still hadn't done very many "flips" and we were still learning the tricks of the trade. We didn't have a lot of extra money to invest so we used a lot of credit cards to buy the materials for the house and Gary did most of the work. So giving the money meant we couldn't pay back our credit cards when we sold the house and it also meant that we could not plan on a half years income we were going to make on the sale. We were a young struggling family with two children and we really needed that money. To me, it was a very hard request from the Lord; even though I questioned what God was telling me, I knew I heard Him speak because I know His voice.

I went home after church and told Gary what I felt the Lord said, and he said, "Well, that's okay; we can give the net profit that we made on the house to the church and still be able to pay the credit cards and expenses accrued during the rehab." My husband is a giver he would give everything we own if I didn't stop him (ha ha). He turned to walk away, got a few steps… and then the Holy Spirit spoke to him and told him to go back and ask me with tears in his eyes, "What did the Lord actually tell you? Did He say to give <u>all</u> the money?" And I said, "Yes, He said to give all the money to the church; yes, even the money we put into the house on the credit cards." At that time, our family income was only about $40,000, and half of that came from flipping a house once a year. It didn't make sense. After we closed on the house and the money was deposited in the bank, we knew we had to give the money to the church building fund.

The next Sunday, with my heart beating and a shaky hand… I wrote out the $24,400 check to the church dropped it in the offering plate and ran to the back of the church (and into the kitchen, out of sight, and bawled my eyes out). Thinking to myself, "Oh, my God, what have we just done?" "This is crazy!" "Was that really you, God?" "Did the devil trick me?" My mind was racing to say the least. We had a close friend that totally ridiculed us for giving all that money to the church when he knew that we were a struggling family with two little kids, but we knew we heard from God and we had to obey His voice. When I don't obey the Lord, I always feel so grieved and, of course, still do to this day.

I must confess: I did complain a lot and talk negatively about God. When the bills came due and I was regretting giving the money, I was not feeling the blessings from heaven. I was scared, but God was always faithful to provide. We had a friend who knew our financial situation and it caused him to leave the church because he didn't think it was right that the church could even accept the money from a young family who didn't have health insurance and couldn't afford some of (what he believed) were the more basic needs of life. But... God was faithful!

I remember one day looking out the window wondering how we were going to come up with the $900.00 for our house payment that was due in a few days. I was praying and singing a song, "I will wait for you" trying to have faith and trust God in my doubt and unbelief. That day we got a phone call for Gary to install a tub. He bid the job and the homeowner gave us $900 in an advance payment before the work started. I felt ashamed for doubting God; God provided and made it happen. Those were tough times, but we never lacked anything.

I heard one minister say, "When God tells you to give something away, and you don't obey, you won't have any joy in keeping the item because (technically) it doesn't belong to you." You will remember that God told you to release it and you will be grieved because you have grieved the Holy Spirit for your disobedience. He never asks for anything without a purpose behind it. I have experienced this before.

Test #3 –Giving up Singing

When we moved to our church, I was about 23 and Gary heard me singing in the car one day and said, "Wow, you can really sing!" I was singing the song "Black Velvet" by Alana Miles (yeah, not very Christian). I didn't know I could sing. I never really thought about it, nor did I care. I sang in the church choir, but I didn't sing during school; I was in the band. I played the flute and then switched to the saxophone. I did belt out a chorus from the movie "Annie" in the band room one time messing around and one of the guys he said, "Wow, you can sing!" I was like "whatever." After I found out that I could sing (in my 20's) and I was really good at it, I became very competitive and jealous of other people that could sing or sing better than me (and I was _not_ worshiping God with my voice). I was more worried about how good I could sing and became competitive and very judgmental of other singers, even though I really did love to worship the Lord and sing to Him.

Like I said earlier, every time my mother would call me up, one of the very first things she would say was, "Have you prayed tongues today?" You can practice (and practice) and sing all you want, but worship is all about the anointing. If you don't have the anointing, then it's not going to matter… and all you'll have is just a pretty voice. "You need the anointing," so I would roll my eyes and say, "Yes, ok, Mom." She was, of course, absolutely right.

One time I was singing in church, and I was asked to sing a special song; I did really good at it and people were very impressed with my voice, and at one point my pastor said "I was his favorite" and commented on how anointed I was. I walked a little taller that day, held my head a little higher and felt pretty good about myself. When I found out I could sing, I would practice and practice and practice and record myself on my little boom box with my tape deck and sing a song 20 to 30 times until I had perfected every note and every nuance of that song. I loved it when people would come up to me afterward saying how beautiful my voice was or how anointed it was. I was finding a lot of self identity in my singing. Eventually over time I joined the worship team and then I was in charge of scheduling special music for church. When I was singing, I was worshiping – but it was more performance and not truly a heart of worship. I became so focused on singing the song as perfectly as I could that I was not really even thinking about ministering to the Lord.

Well, one day, I was back home in Wisconsin visiting my mom; she was dying of ovarian cancer, and I went to be with her and help her in her final days. Now, that's a whole other story. I was running on her treadmill because it was winter time and it was freezing cold with snow on the ground. When I was on the treadmill, I heard the Lord say, "I want you to lay down singing, I want to use you in a greater way and I can't where you're at right now." What??!! Once again, I couldn't believe what I was hearing, but I knew that I knew… I heard from God and when God speaks He doesn't change his mind. To give up singing was truly… to lay down my life at this time in my life.

I remember when I told Gary. He understood, and he believed that I'd heard from the Lord, so we went and sat down with our pastor. Pastor really questioned me about laying it down because I had a gift and I had an anointing. I told him I know it didn't make sense to me either, but I knew I had heard God and _I had to do it_. Now this decision to lay down singing took me a long while (between when the Lord told me, and before I actually obeyed Him). I mean… laying it down meant not singing at church, not doing specials, and not being on stage, but (of course) I still sang at home. It probably took me a year to lay it down; yep, stubborn and bull headed I was. I didn't want to give it up, but every time I got up to sing, I was absolutely miserable and felt so grieved; and every time I got up to sing, I knew what God told me (how I was to lay it down) and I knew that I was in disobedience. I finally surrendered, and when I told my worship leaders, they questioned it, but they just needed to know that I had heard the voice of God and I had their support.

The first Sunday I went to church and sat in the congregation, I was so nervous, I felt like a fish out of water because I was not on up on stage singing with the worship team. I felt like all eyes were on me and what people were thinking: "Why is she not up there singing?" It felt so awkward and so out of touch. That Sunday after church, when I got home, I fell on my hands and knees on our back porch and started balling. I actually felt like I cried my whole insides out of me. I was literally sobbing and grieving like I had lost someone (pretty pathetic of me). I cried so deeply; I was heaving and hyperventilating and losing my breath from crying so hard from giving up this gift – this thing that I absolutely loved and adored. I realized that I had become my idol over my God and my King. Singing affirmed me in ministry and gave me identity. I loved the affirmation.

During this time (before the Lord had me lay down

my singing), I had read a lot about Abraham and his
sacrifice to Isaac on the altar and how God
provided a ram in the bush and that God provided a
way.

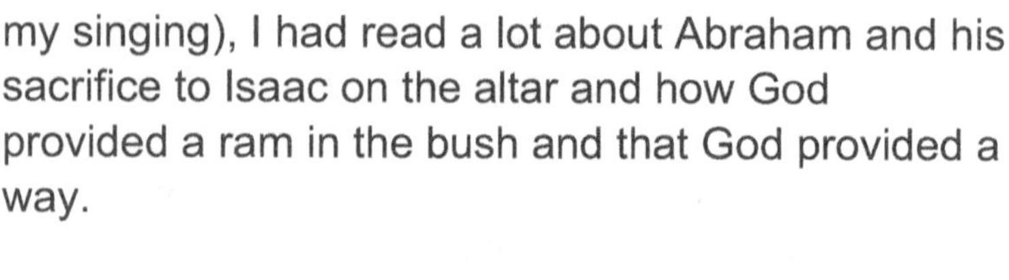

*Genesis 22:2 "And he said, Take now thy son, thine
only son Isaac, whom thou lovest, and get thee into
the land of Moriah; and offer him there for a burnt
offering upon one of the mountains which I will tell
thee of." (KJV)*

God doesn't ask us to give up anything just for us to
give it; there is always a purpose behind it! At the
time we're laying it down – crucifying our own self
love and our own flesh – it seems horrible, but all
the things that I gave up… I don't miss them at all…
once I finally do surrender them. God made it so
hard for me not to not obey. I mean He was on me
hard, probably because I did want more of Him. He
knew it and He pursued me like a loving Father.
Thank God! Of course, I do sing again now and
lead worship; however, those three years of time I
spent alone worshiping God after I laid down
performance singing, taught me… what it truly
means to worship Him… and I am forever changed

for it. During my time alone, I learned and have grown to love prophetic worship and spontaneous singing to the Lord.

- I WANTED MORE OF GOD -

The personal revival I had was orchestrated completely by God. I wanted more of Him! He heard my hearts cry and *He* pursued… and pursued me. He knew I had to lay down these specific things in my life. He wanted it more at the time probably than I did. That's why, even though it took me seemingly forever to obey, He kept pressing me and pressing me. I was not very willing but eventually I was obedient. What's my point? It was all Him anyway. It always is… and He gets all the glory. I cannot stick my chest out and say look at what I gave up for God like I'm someone super spiritual. It was all Him!

There will be other tests along the way that God asks of us, or should I say me. I remember we had another house on the market and God told me that the house would not sell until I gave up singing again. What?! I'm thinking, this is so "me" thinking this, and that is completely ridiculous. I couldn't believe God said that, but sure enough… after I laid down the singing the house sold.

I believe that these three tests were opportunities for me to show the Lord that I was serious about pursuing Him. He says if you seek me with all your heart you will find me.

——————————— ✦ ———————————

*Jeremiah 29:13 "And ye shall seek me, and find me, when ye shall search for me with all your heart".
(KJV)*

——————————— ✦ ———————————

I wanted Him more than the things He asked of me. I wanted to obey Him more than those things I really wanted, and deep, deep down inside – I just had to obey him. Like the scripture in Matthew says:

——————————— ✦ ———————————

Matthew 22:14. "Many are called but few are chosen" (KJV)

——————————— ✦ ———————————

As I mentioned earlier, I like to say, "Many are called, but few are willing to pay the price to be chosen." I paid a price in this and God chose me. So worth it all!

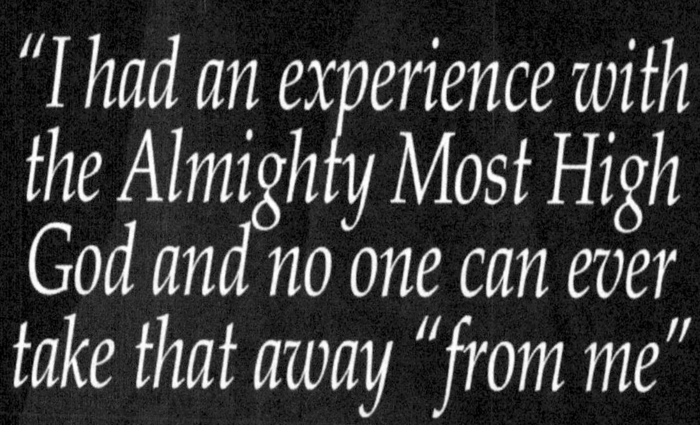

"I had an experience with the Almighty Most High God and no one can ever take that away "from me"

-Tracey McReynolds

Chapter 3
When God showed up

On Sunday, January 20, 2002, our Bishop had come to speak at church again. I don't actually remember what the sermon was about, but at the end of the service I was very compelled that I needed to stay at the church after everyone left and just worship God and pray. It was the most overwhelming compelling feeling that I've ever had. So I was "fit to be tied" during service, very distracted with this overwhelming feeling, and I knew something was up… but I had no idea what.

On that particular Sunday, we had keys to the church because we had security duty and, of course, God knew that. The miracle about this event included this: there was a football game on, but Gary agreed to stay with me when I told him I just have to stay at the church. My kids were about 8 and 10 years old at the time. We locked the doors, turn off all the lights, and then I went up to the altar in the gymnasium (since that is where we were having church). I stood at the altar (being very compelled to be there) and after about three minutes the Fire of God descended upon me. It went from the top of my head down to my feet and consumed me. Oh my God!!! What is this???!!!

✦

Matthew 3:11-12 "I indeed baptize you with water unto repentance, but he that cometh after me is mightier than I, whose shoes I am not worthy to bear: he shall baptize you with the Holy Ghost, and with fire: 12 Whose fan is in his hand, and he will thoroughly purge his floor, and gather his wheat into the garner; but he will burn up the chaff with unquenchable fire." (KJV)

✦

I had been born again and saved for over 20 years, yet I had *never* felt that type of power or presence of God in my entire Christian life. I never even knew it existed. I had read about it, I had heard about the fire, but I had never experienced it. It was very, very, very intense, very gut-wrenching, so much pressure on my physical body. I felt like I was a burning person on fire. I was flipping and flopping around and screaming while I was rolling around on the stage under this incredible power from God. I was breathing super hard almost hyperventilating with rapid breathing. My heart and spirit were on fire, it felt like God was burning something out of me and at the same time – I was being "branded" and marked that I was truly His. My shirt and skirt were riding up because of all my flipping and flopping around. I ended up on the floor shaking uncontrollably and thinking "Oh my God, is this a demon? Wait no, that can't be, I am a born again Christian, I love God". Admittedly, I was scared and feeling completely out of control; I could do nothing to stop what was happening because I was totally overcome at that moment by the Holy Ghost. I was then thinking simultaneously, this is the same thing I have read in books about what happens in revival and testimonies of what people talk about when they say "God turn it off, turn it off." So said "God, turn it off" I can't take anymore". This unbearable intensity lasted for about the longest 15 minutes of my life (though I'm not sure how long it lasted). I was thinking, "Wow, this awesome God of the universe is barely touching me with his pinky finger – if even that – maybe a fallen hair from His head. He has so much power." It was as if an angel from Heaven threw a ball of Holy Ghost fire on me. All I can say is… wow! After the intensity diminished to where it was almost bearable, it was still several more hours before Gary could drag me to the car because His presence was still all over me.

I'm so very glad God poured out His Spirit on me when it was just Gary, my kids and me. I'm so glad no one else was around. People would have freaked out to say the least. Heck, I was freaked out! The crazy thing about all this is no one prayed for me and no one laid hands on me. During this period of time in the mid 1990's, the Brownsville revival was going on in Pensacola, Florida. I wanted to go so bad; however, I never made it down there, but God decided I would have my own personal revival without needing to leave town.   **Thank you, Jesus**!

Again, I like to say that statement Leonard Ravenhill says, "A man with an experience is never at the mercy of a man with an argument." People have judged the manifestations of God, but I want to say: when the creator of the heavens and the universe who spoke the worlds into existence, the same One that raised Christ from the dead, split the Red Sea and has done miracle after miracle… touches our mere mortal flesh, we will react under His power and His power is dynamic and His power is incredible and His power is amazing! I had an experience with the Almighty Most High God and *no one can ever take that away from me*, I mean no one can tell me God isn't real and what happened to me wasn't real. People can try and argue with me and talk me out of it. That will NEVER happen! I was there and my Husband and kids knew it was real.

I walked away that day from church thinking how God does really love me. I wrote it down in my journal. I would *never* be the same. I mean… how could I? After what just happened, I was marked for life. He saw me, He sees me, and He knows my comings and goings. He orchestrated that encounter just for me. I felt very, very special. Here I was praying that one day He would touch me; I was hungry for Him and I wanted more of Him… and then it happened! When His fire comes, it comes to burn out our self, our flesh, heal our hearts and also to empower and anoint. One touch from God is all we need. His word says He will send his refining fire and His fuller's soap. That day I was truly stamped with the seal of the promised Holy Spirit.

✦

Ephesians 1:13 "And because of him, when you *who are not Jews* heard the revelation of truth, you believed in the wonderful news of salvation. Now we have been stamped with the seal of the promised Holy Spirit." (The Passion Translation)

✦

Malachi 3:2 "But who may abide the day of his coming? and who shall stand when he appeareth? for he is like a refiner's fire, and like fullers' soap."
(KJV)

✦

Another time the Holy Spirit was poured out with the baptism of fire was in the upper room. In Acts Chapter 2:

✦

"And when the day of Pentecost was fully come, they were all with one accord in one place. 2 And suddenly there came a sound from heaven as of a rushing mighty wind, and it filled all the house where they were sitting. 3 And there appeared unto them cloven tongues like as of fire, and it sat upon each of them. 4 And they were all filled with the Holy Ghost, and began to speak with other tongues, as the Spirit gave them utterance.

5 And there were dwelling at Jerusalem Jews, devout men, out of every nation under heaven. 6 Now when this was noised abroad, the multitude came together, and were confounded, because that every man heard them speak in his own language. 7 And they were all amazed and marvelled, saying one to another, Behold, are not all these which speak Galilaeans? 8 And how hear we every man in our own tongue, wherein we were born? 9 Parthians, and Medes, and Elamites, and the dwellers in Mesopotamia, and in Judaea, and Cappadocia, in Pontus, and Asia, 10 Phrygia, and Pamphylia, in Egypt, and in the parts of Libya about Cyrene, and *strangers of Rome, Jews and proselytes, ¹¹ Cretes and Arabians, we do hear them speak in our tongues the wonderful works of God. ¹² And they were all amazed, and were in doubt, saying one to another, What meaneth this? ¹³ Others mocking said, these men are full of new wine.*

¹⁴ But Peter, standing up with the eleven, lifted up his voice, and said unto them, Ye men of Judaea, and all ye that dwell at Jerusalem, be this known unto you, and hearken to my words: ¹⁵ For these are not drunken, as ye suppose, seeing it is but the third hour of the day. ¹⁶ But this is that which was spoken by the prophet Joel;

¹⁷ "'In the last days, God says,
  'I will pour out my Spirit on all people.
Your sons and daughters will prophesy,
    your young men will see visions,
    your old men will dream dreams.
¹⁸ Even on my servants, both men and women,
    I will pour out my Spirit in those days,
    and they will prophesy.
¹⁹ I will show wonders in the heavens above
    and signs on the earth below,
    blood and fire and billows of smoke.
²⁰ The sun will be turned to darkness
    and the moon to blood
    before the coming of the great and glorious day of the Lord.
²¹ And everyone who calls

✦

The disciples waited for the promise of the Holy Spirit to be baptized with the Holy Spirit and fire, and there is no doubt that they encountered God in the upper room. I was waiting on God in a large empty gymnasium and I encountered Him. I was waiting in faith with expectation not even knowing what to expect – and He came and met me right where I was at in a specific time and place, set aside just for me. How amazing!

Again, needless to say, that was an encounter with God that I will never ever forget. I felt so loved by God. I called my mother and told her; I don't really remember what her response was, but from this day forward every time God would touch me like that and I told her, she would always say "Did you have another episode?" I'd say, "Really Mom? It's not an episode. God is showing up, God is touching me, and this is an encounter with the Holy Spirit." It was annoying to say the least.

From that day since, after the Lord touched me in that church gymnasium – it's like His hand is still upon me to this day 19 years later it is never lifted. It's almost like a cloak has been put on me. He got closer to me… a lot closer. It's hard to explain in natural terms.

I remember going to the grocery store a day or so later (after the encounter at the church) and God's presence was so heavy on me I felt jittery, I could barely walk; I had to come home. I just didn't understand what was going on so I called Gary and he thought it was such a fluke thing; he thought I was crazy and quite frankly so did I. This presence of God upon me went on for one day, then two days, and then continued for days and days, I really didn't understand it. I thought for sure that was a onetime encounter. I had no idea His presence would linger like it did. This was all so new to me.

Let me say: we put God in a box. There are levels in God; He is vast, and He is so amazing; He is beyond description – beyond comprehension. He says in His Word: My thoughts are not your thoughts, My ways are not your ways, My ways are higher.

✦

Isaiah 55:8-9 "For my thoughts are not your thoughts, neither are your ways my ways, saith the Lord. For as the heavens are higher than the earth, so are my ways higher than your ways, and my thoughts than your thoughts." (KJV)

✦

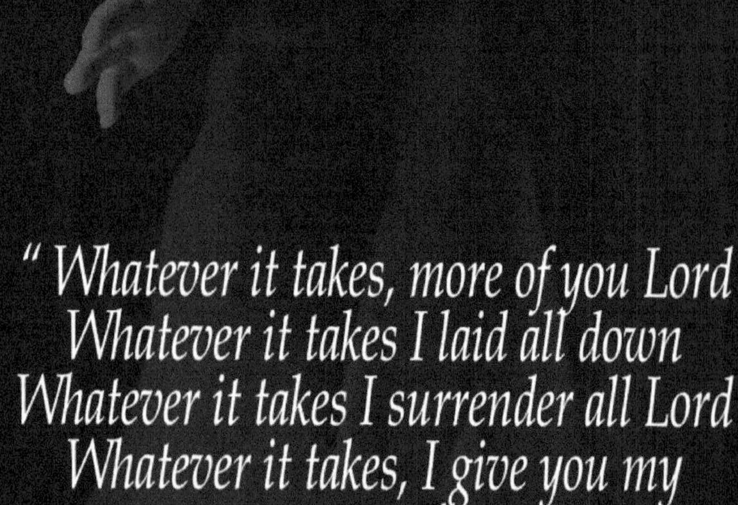

" Whatever it takes, more of you Lord
Whatever it takes I laid all down
Whatever it takes I surrender all Lord
Whatever it takes, I give you my
crowns"

-Tracey McReynolds

Chapter 4
Early Days In My Revival

After my encounter at the Church, God's presence did wane a little, I don't exactly remember. Life got back to normal (or so I thought), but I had no idea this was just the beginning… and a lot more was to come. A few months after the encounter at our church, I had another encounter that I was not expecting at all. Like I said, I thought God's presence that I experienced only comes like that once in a person's lifetime.

One particular evening Gary and I had been fighting and arguing, nothing at all spiritual was happening whatsoever that I remember.   We went to bed and we were talking and as I was lying in bed… my whole body went like numb and I had a tingling sensation all over me and I thought, "Oh my God, I'm having a heart attack" (because Gary says that I always worry too much) and I thought, "Well here it is, I'm dying" – but what actually happened was: the presence of the Lord was coming upon me and it was quite spectacular. I (or should I say)… "We" were totally caught off guard. God is showing up again! Wait! Stuff like this happens to Christians? How come I've never heard about this? Is this normal? God… is this real?

I was very humbled by His presence, to say the least. For the next two hours while the tangible presence of the Lord was in our bedroom; we spent the next two hours praying, repenting and crying about everything we could ever think of that we had done, including everything that we thought we could have done that would be grievous and displeasing to the Lord. I mean… God was in our bedroom. We were awe struck, shocked, humbled and honored all at the same time.

The encounters kept coming, and each one was different. I remember another time so specific: I was sitting at the piano and worshiping, I know earlier I had said the Lord asked me to lay down my music and my singing (at church), but I still loved to worship and sing, so I had one of my dear super talented friends teach me three chords on the piano because I really, really wanted to sing to the Lord and worship Him (and I still do). So, I purchased a piano and then eventually over time began writing songs unto the Lord and truly became a worshiper. It was very common for me to spend 3-4 hours at a time sitting at the piano and that is where I became a true worshipper of Him and learned what it meant to really worship.
These are a couple songs I penned in worship to the

Lord. I'm not a song writer, per se; these songs just came from my heart to Him. I currently only sing them to Him. Maybe one day… I'll share them.

<u>"Whatever it Takes"</u>

Whatever it takes, More of You Lord
Whatever it takes, I lay it all down
Whatever it takes, I surrender my all Lord
Whatever it takes, I give you my crowns
To know You , to have You more in my life
Your presence, Your Power, Your Glory divine
Whatever it Takes, I'll take up my cross Lord
Whatever it Takes, I'll Give You my whole life
Whatever it takes, I'll pay the price Lord
Whatever it takes, It's no Sacrifice.
Whatever it takes, More of Your presence
Whatever it takes, More of You Lord
Whatever it Takes, I'm willing Lord
Whatever it Takes, I surrender my All
Whatever it Takes, That you would increase, till I become nothing at all.

<u>"Come Away"</u>

Your Spirit's, calling unto me
Seek Me, Seek Me, My Child
Run to me, Run to me, My Child
Come Away, Come Away, Come Away, My
Child
Your Spirit's, calling unto me
Draw to me, Draw to me my child
I am here, I am near, my child
Seek Me you'll find Me, Run to Me find me
Come away, Come Away
Leave all behind you
Seek me, I'm right here by you
Come Away, Come Away
Come Away, Separate
Come Away, Don't hesitate
Come Away

The Fear of the Lord

Then one day, the Holy reverential fear of the Lord came into my bedroom while I was worshipping at the piano. The kind of presence the Bible talks about in Isaiah:

✦

Isaiah 2:10 " Enter into the rock, and hide in the dust, from the terror of the LORD And the glory of His majesty." (NKJV)

✦

This particular day, I experienced the fear of the Lord – where His presence is so Holy and you know He is so pure and perfect and full of light. In this moment, you are very aware and know that: you are mere carnal flesh, you are mortal, you are grass, and you're so glad you are covered in the Blood of Jesus. I have to say, I was kind of scared. It was very, very intense. All I could do was get on my face, lay prostrate and cry out to Him. I cried out "Holy, Holy, Holy. God, You are so Holy." I mean, I was in the presence of majesty and holiness; I was in the presence of The King of Kings. It was so real, it was so tangible, it was *nothing* like I've ever experienced in life up to this point. I wish I could have sunk down into the hardwood floors that I was laying prostrate on. I experienced His presence this way just this one time.

I've thought very often if this 'presence of the Lord' would invade our churches and/or come into our homes, the body of Christ would stop compromising and get serious and stop playing church. I have asked the Lord: "Why don't You come into the Church with your Holy pure presence like I experienced?" I haven't gotten an answer from Him yet, so I am here to tell you about my own experience. When and if God moves on the body of Christ this way, people will weep and wail for their hidden sins and their wrong living. They will repent for everything and anything they have done or thought about doing. They will see their sin and know that they are mere carnal filthy flesh. They will never be the same. I personally think the body of Christ needs this kind of wake up call. I think we forgot how Holy and powerful God is… and He has become too familiar to us. We really do forget He is Holy! Sometimes I think we need a chastening from our Father to get us back in line. God has many expressions. I have experienced a lot of them… and this is one I will never forget.

I am not just bringing glory to manifestations I experienced in my encounters with the Holy Spirit – I was going after HIM! You have to understand: this was all completely so new to me and I was pretty much all alone. I had no one else I could speak to that even understood what was going on.

I am here to tell you that God is so real and He will draw near to you as you seek and draw near to Him… but there is a purpose for the touch of God. He sends His anointing and power <u>on</u> you so it flows <u>from</u> you onto others. God is not a respecter of persons. You can get as close to God as you want. How bad do you want Him? And how hungry are you for Him? He is looking for hungry hearts seeking after Him. God wants to be wanted, and He goes where He is wanted!

Another Whole New Experience

During this time, my mom had ovarian cancer; it was a very difficult time for her; but she loved God and still pursued Him. She was coming to visit us in Virginia and we planned to attend a conference in Washington D.C. with her. I remember it was in June, it was one week before she came, and I was feeling super weird. It's like everything on my body hurt – but it didn't hurt. I could feel (and was aware of) everything on my physical body, my eyelashes, the nail on my pinky toe, my ear lobes, etc. Weird, I know! I can't explain it. After the Lord encountered me in January, His hand was very heavy upon me. I mean, it literally felt this weight, like someone with their arm hanging on you; it was very tangible… knowing that His hand was upon me.

There is a Hebrew word "Shekinah" that means: "dwelling or settling of the divine presence of God." Many people say "the Shekinah Glory of God" to describe this presence. Well, it sure seemed like the Shekinah presence of the Lord was visiting me.

✦

Revelation 21:3 "And I heard a loud voice from heaven saying, "Behold, the tabernacle of God is with men, and He will dwell with them, and they shall be His people. God Himself will be with them and be their God." (NKJV)

✦

So this particular week, I was feeling super weird and out-of-sorts. Really can't explain it. Something was definitely up and probably getting ready to happen. My mom came to Virginia to stay with us and we went to the End Time Handmaidens conference in Washington D.C. The End-Time Handmaidens are radical intercessors for the Lord founded by the late Gwen Shaw. To become a member of the End-Time Handmaidens, you have to go on a 21 day diluted vegetable juice or fruit fast (which mom did).

My Mother was always pursuing Jesus. She diligently sought Him, and she would travel from conference to conference. Before she passed in January of 2003, she was studying Judaism and was always listening to preaching and constantly praying in tongues. I also want to mention, God was so close to me during this time of my mom's death and He definitely showed me that He is the Comforter. I sobbed for my mom only one time sitting in her bedroom back at her home while she was in the hospital (in hospice), and never really cried other than that. I lived in Virginia and she lived in Wisconsin, and I'm sure it helped (somewhat) that we didn't live close to each other. If we had been closer, I'm sure It would have been harder on me. She always wanted me to live closer to her, just like any loving mother. I would always tell her, "Mom, that's not Gods will." Well, she knew, but she didn't like it. His grace was and is truly amazing and was resting upon me when she passed. As I was crying while sitting in her bedroom, I literally felt tangible arms wrap around and hold me. I was being held by something supernatural… and it was amazing! The Scriptures came alive to me during the death of my mother – how God is our loving Father, our Comforter and how His amazing grace sustains us in difficult times. Just like His Word says.

Anyway, I specifically remember at the conference during one evening service where Tommy Tenney was ministering on Isaiah 54:1 ...Oh, Barren woman... I don't really remember the whole message and I remember he gave an altar call, but I didn't go forward. I didn't feel like I should because I was feeling super weird again. I guess I felt like something was getting ready to happen, like the presence of God was going to move on me again (and I think I told my mom I was feeling weird). I think the whole auditorium went forward and my mom and I were the only ones who stayed in our seats (there were probably about 900 people there). As I was standing by my seat, I felt this power of the Holy Spirit suddenly come down upon me with this surge of power – like a lightning bolt; it was a suddenly and it really caught me of guard. I screamed, I was thrown back into the chairs and landed on the floor, then I knocked over my mom's iced tea (which got all over me and on my white shawl) and then I began this groaning out of my belly. When I was blasted back into the chairs, I was not hurt; it all happened so fast. I believe it was in this service and at that moment that God graced me and called me to intercession. It says in Romans;

Romans 8:26 "Likewise the Spirit also helpeth our infirmities: for we know not what we should pray for as we ought: but the Spirit itself maketh intercession for us with groanings which cannot be uttered." (KJV)

I had never experienced anything like that before. This groaning came up out of my spirit; I was compelled to do it. _I had to do it_! I was thinking… what the heck is this? I felt like I was giving birth. I was moaning and felt like pushing something out of me (in the Spirit). Again, I was naive and untaught about all these things. Ironically, no one came over that I remember and asked if I was alright or what was going on. No one thought it was strange (which I am not surprised being that we were with a group of radical intercessors anyway). I think my mom was completely caught off guard too. She seemed unsure of herself – and helpless. After that night began a whole other level of encounters with God.

People always say God is a gentleman… and He is. As I said, God has many expressions from what I've experienced. God is gentlemanly when he woos you in the moment you become a born-again, as well when you are a baby Christian and [are] so excited; He is very, very patient and gentle with you (or should I say me). But as you grow in the Lord, He shows [more of] Himself and can reveal Himself as a stern Father. The Bible says God chastens those that He loves. And when he comes as a stern Father, it doesn't seem very gentlemanly. I have experienced the displeasure of the Lord a few times. I have had the Lord yell at me for my disobedience, bad attitude and negative speech. When you have surrendered all – God takes you at your word. And for me, there were and still are things that I'm stubborn and obstinate about and Holy Spirit will scold me, but He always does it in a way to bring restoration. After all, the Bible says his kindness leads to repentance. What am I saying here? **Stop making God... the God of <u>your</u> understanding**. He is gentlemanly and He can be a] harmless dove, but that is only one of his [many] attributes; He doesn't always move in this way. God will offend the mind to reveal the heart. He will compel you do things your flesh does not want you to do. There have been times that He's told me to forgive but I didn't want to. My flesh didn't want to do it but the Holy Spirit pressed me (and kept pressing me). And you know why he pressed me? Because he knows that unforgiveness is a sin. He desires instant obedience from us.

After I attended the End Time Handmaiden Conference meeting with my mother, I began to get this groaning more often although I had no idea what was happening to me. I would be sitting, eating breakfast, and I could hardly sit still in my seat. I would feel jittery and have to go to my bedroom, and I would be shaking due to the heavy presence of God on me and start groaning. I had no idea what was going on. I had never been taught or trained about any of this kind of stuff. I did not learn about this in my church or Bible school. I knew my Mom didn't know about it either because, when we would talk on the phone, she would always ask me if I had any more "episodes." Episodes? That is what she called them, so I began to search online and read books to try and figure out what God was doing with me.

During this time, while the Holy Spirit was so heavy on me, I would also have these encounters during the church service. I was so sensitive to the presence of the Lord. I would fall out on the floor during the service, I would shake on the gymnasium floor, and I was being stared at; I became a spectacle and I did not like it. When I fell, out it happened so fast; one minute I was sitting there listening and the next minute I was on the floor under the power of the Holy Ghost. I know people were judging me and criticizing me very harshly. I mean – I probably would have too. I looked very strange. This was not normal behavior even though we attended a Full-Gospel, Spirit-Filled, Pentecostal church. So I got smart. As I began to feel the Holy Spirit coming upon me, I would go to the back of the church or in the restroom so people would stop looking at me. I was being judged (and harshly at that). I knew it was God, but I really didn't know much more than that. I thought the church members would be happy for me or at least curious and ask me what was happening? But most were just critical. (shock, shock) But there was one dear senior prayer warrior who would come up to me with all of her southern bell sweetness and say," I just love hearing those drums" referring to how my feet would bang on the floor in rapid fire under the powerful shaking of God's power and presence.

Let me also say as another reminder: I am not bringing glory to the manifestations. *I am bringing glory to God that is a result of His manifestations upon me*.

It's not about the shaking or groaning. Manifestations are a result of an all powerful God touching our frail, weak, mortal flesh. When the all-consuming fire of the Holy Spirit touches you, your physical body *will* react. If all they are – are manifestations and there is no heart change in someone, it was probably all flesh. I went after Him. I wanted more of Him!

Eventually, God sent a new couple to our church. Due to a family crisis, they were coming back from missionary work from Brazil (but prior to that they were very heavily involved in the Brownsville Revival in Pensacola, Florida). My friend and her husband were a part of that revival for three years. She was not offended and even seemed to understand all of these experiences and manifestations I was having and, in fact, acted very nonchalant. She told me what was happening to me was very common in Revival. She asked me, "Do you know what is happening to you?" I said, "No, please, please tell me!" She said, "God is using you as an intercessor." I said "What? An intercessor? What exactly does that mean?" She would go on to explain how intercessors at the Brownsville Revival would be laying on the floor shaking, groaning and crying because they were praying for lost souls, and for the Kingdom, and whatever other things the Holy Spirit would have them pray for. She became my best friend during this season. She was the only one who really understood what was going on.   I talked to her a lot about how I was feeling and what was going on because I did not understand it, at all.

Love-Sick for Jesus

During this time of personal revival and intercession, I was also becoming enamored with and absolutely love- sick for my Lord. *Yes! Love -sick! I had to be in His presence;* I had to sit in His presence; I had to worship Him; I had to be with Him. I would be at work all day and I would come home miserable from missing Him – and so in love – desperately waiting to be alone in my prayer closet with the Lord. I would get in the door, run upstairs to my bedroom, fall to my knees and I would cry and cry because I missed him so bad during the day. Again, I didn't know I could feel this way towards Jesus. I mean… totally Love-sick for Him. I mean… smitten. The scripture below is very accurate and best describes me.

____

__________________   ✦   __________________

Psalm 63:1-4 (The Passion Translation)
"O God of my life, I'm lovesick for you in this weary
wilderness. I thirst with the deepest longings to love
you more, with cravings in my heart that can't be
described.
Such yearning grips my soul for you, my God!
² I'm energized every time I enter
your heavenly sanctuary to seek more of your power
and drink in more of your glory.
³ For your tender mercies mean more to me than life
itself. How I love and praise you, God!
⁴ Daily I will worship you passionately and with all
my heart.
My arms will wave to you like banners of praise."

__________________   ✦   __________________

Little Girl

During this period of being love-sick and desperate I
was longing for God as my Father.   I had an ache in
my heart that longed to be filled by Him. I became
like a desperate little girl wanting her Daddy! I
would imagine myself as this little girl in a light
colored pink dress with black patent leather shoes
with white ankle socks, on my tiptoes with my arms
up in the air saying, "Pick me up, Daddy", "Hold me
Daddy", "I want you Daddy", "I need you Daddy."

There was just something in me that needed the affirmation and love of my Father God. Like most of us, we didn't get the affirmation or love that we needed or wanted from our earthly fathers, and we still have a longing for our "Daddy". There are over 1500 times when the word father (i.e. father, father's, fathers, fathers') occurs in the Bible. The word Father (in regard to God) occurs even more than the word Pastor. We get our identity, our strength and provision from our Fathers. I heard one preacher say, "We need more Fathers and less teachers in the Body of Christ."

I've said there are many expressions of God. He is all things to us, and He meets all our needs. We all have areas in our lives that are lacking things that only God can fill, and He comes to us when and how we need Him. In certain moments, when I needed Him to be a Father, He was/is my "Daddy God". No one else can do what He can do for me. We can take comfort and know that – anytime and in any place and in any circumstance – we can call upon God and He is right in there in the midst of us, even when we need Him to be our "Daddy"!

The Hall Tree

Another time, during this period of being absolutely love-sick for God, I wanted to express my love to Him. It was hard to say how deeply I was feeling about Him. It was beyond words. This may seem a little weird, BUT… while I was worshipping, I remembered the story of the women with the alabaster box (Luke 7) how she washed Jesus' feet with her tears and anointed His feet with the costly oil and then wiped His feet with her hair. There was a hall tree or coat rack in the room where I was worshipping and of course I was all alone. Thank goodness. The hall tree had four "feet". I got down on my hands and knees and in that moment (in my imagination) those feet were the feet of Jesus, and I was compelled to show the same sentiment as the women did in the Bible. As I was weeping, I then wiped my hair on those "feet." I told Jesus, "I love you and I have to demonstrate this love that I feel inside, down in the deepest parts of my heart." Remember: God looks at the heart. I felt the pleasure of the Lord in this intimate moment. Too many people are concerned with what other people think when it comes to worshipping God. Just worship God by how you're feeling in your heart in that moment and stop being concerned about what it looks like. But (just like me) don't be afraid to step out and do something different when you're alone because it's your chance to push the boundaries of your expression, especially when your heart is to please Him in your worship.

Having A Clean Heart

During this time, God had to get my heart right in a lot of areas, including folks at the church I had gossiped about and spoke negatively about. He impressed upon me to go and confess any thought I had in my heart toward them. There was even a girl I was jealous of (who I thought sang better than me) and I had to go confess to her and get this jealously up out of my spirit. It was very humbling to say the least. Every time I went to someone to ask for forgiveness, even though I hadn't done anything to them personally, I would be so nervous and had butterflies in my stomach. They were usually caught off guard, but I had to do it. I had to have clean hands and a pure heart toward them, and most of all – towards the Lord. I could not have anything in my heart that hindered my walk with the Lord. I could not have sin in my heart toward my brother and sister in Christ. God calls us to be holy as He is Holy. I had to be clean in front of man and most of all clean before God, because He saw my heart condition. The Bible says, "Man looks at the outward appearance, but the Lord looks at the heart" (1 Sam. 16:7).

1 Samuel 16:7 _"But the_ LORD _said to Samuel, "Do not look at his appearance or at his physical stature, because I have refused him. For_
_t̶he_ LORD _does not see as man sees; for man looks at the outward appearance, but the_ LORD _looks at the heart." (KJV)_

Apologizing To My Pastor

I remember one service we had on Sunday night at our church. Sundays nights are usually smaller crowds. Thank God. "They" say you can tell how popular the <u>church</u> is by how big the crowd on Sunday mornings, how popular the <u>pastor</u> is by the crowd on Sunday nights, and how popular <u>Jesus</u> is by the crowd on Wednesdays. Anyway, the Holy Spirit was really moving. While I was sitting in my seat, I felt so strongly by the Lord to go up in front of the church and repent for speaking badly about my Pastor. "Again, really God? Why are you making me do this?? No! Please!" I mean, I had major nerves about doing this. I argued with the Lord for sometime before I surrendered and got up and confessed in front of the entire congregation about speaking badly about my Pastor. He was looking at me wide-eyed when I got up to start speaking. He was probably as nervous about me getting up there as I was, I'm sure.

Gary and I were leaders in the church, so I think it set an example for a lot of the people in the church. I asked pastor for forgiveness of those things that I had spoken behind his back about decisions he had made, how he handled things or just judging him for not being the leader I thought he should be. I think he was quite shocked when I confessed this. It was very humbling, to say the least. Nothing spectacular happened that night after I went up front, except I obeyed God and that's all that really mattered. Really, only Heaven knows. I didn't look at anyone in their seats, but I know all eyes were looking at me and I'm sure you could have heard a pin drop. I mean, how many people go up in front of a church congregation and confess the secret things of the heart or tell the things that you have spoken in secret or gossiped about their pastor, especially when you're a leader in the church. Do we need more of this in our churches today? I know we do.

✦

Psalms 105:15 "Saying, Touch not mine anointed, and do my prophets no harm." (KJV)

✦

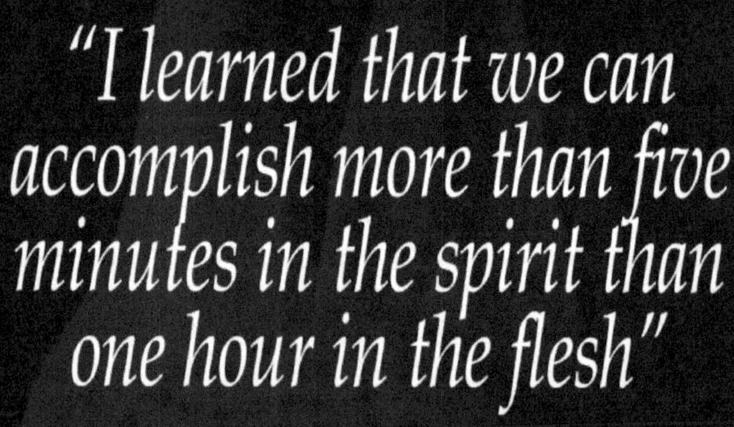

"I learned that we can accomplish more than five minutes in the spirit than one hour in the flesh"

-Tracey McReynolds

Chapter 5
The Intercession Starts

The longest I've spent alone in prayer was twelve hours and most of those twelve hours was in worship. But on average I would spend 3 to 4 hours a day in prayer. I wish I could say I do that now, but back during the center of my revival it was 3 to 4 hours every day. About 90% of the time during my prayer time was spent worshiping Him, sitting in His presence and being still. Only about 10% of the time was spent asking and petitioning the Lord.

There are different reasons for prayer and intercession. I knew when it was time to war in the Spirit. I knew when it was time to intercede for others. I knew when it was time to petition the Lord. I learned that we can accomplish more in five minutes in the Spirit than one hour in the flesh. He longs for fellowship with us. That's why I think I spent most my time in worship and just being still in His presence.

I thought, how can any minister of the gospel be effective and not spend time in prayer?

During this time of intercession, I was the most fulfilled and content I've even been in my entire life, yet I was judged very, very harshly for the outward manifestations and they did *look* crazy. Some people told my husband that the African carvings he brought back from Liberia were demon possessed and they got on me, but what they didn't know (because no one ever asked) was that I was on fire for Christ and I spent hours and hours in His presence becoming passionate for Him, and passionate for the things of God and the Kingdom of God, and I would weep for lost souls. I was ridiculed by my own Spirit-filled Charismatic church, but they didn't know what was going on (just like I didn't know what was going on).

My pastor called my husband and me into his office one day and we discussed what was going on with me. He said "You can have "this" or leadership." I was absolutely heartbroken. But for me, it was a no-brainer; I chose those encounters and personal revival with God. Gary was willing to forgo leadership in our church as well because he saw the transformation from my apathetic, mediocre Christian life into a sold out, on fire, follower of Christ.

I wanted so badly to be able to transfer all of this intense pent-up passion and presence of the Lord onto others. So, during one church service, actually,

I asked if I could lay hands on everybody; I wanted to give it away, and many people came forward and wanted a touch from the Lord. I don't know if anybody got touched, but I ended up praying for a lot of people. Still to this day, I love to impart the incredible presence of the Holy Spirit so that people can encounter His powerful presence (that I was experiencing on almost a daily basis). I do pray for folks and His presence shows up, but I want them to experience the fire of God's manifest presence, I want to see miracles and healing, and I want to see people set free from all kinds of bondages. In Jesus Name!

Gary and I had a lawn care business during at the time of my personal revival. The Spirit of intercession was so heavy on me at times that – even while I was mowing – I had to get off of the mower and get in the truck and lay across the seat where I would shake, groan and pray in tongues until the Spirit of intercession lifted. No matter what kind of work I was doing… when Holy Spirit would come upon me… I had to stop what I was doing and pray. I was unable to do anything else anyway. It was overwhelming to say the least. When it's time to pray, it's time to pray. Lives may be at stake. Only God knows. This is still true today, even though it's been 19 years since this began. This intense burden to pray and intercede comes upon me and I am compelled to yield until this laboring in the Spirit is complete.

This is a spontaneous prophetic song that I started singing after I had finished warfare Intercession.

<u>I had Joy and Victory!</u>
I am a warrior
Darkness will not prevail,
When in the Spirit I groan and travail
I am a warrior
Demons will flee when I'm down on praying on my knees
I am a warrior
The kingdom of Darkness will not stand
 because I'm under His command
I am a warrior, A Holy Ghost warrior, A Praying warrior
Power and principalities will flee when He answers the plea from His warrior
A mighty warrior!

I already know what you're thinking: this girl is weird; this is crazy; could this really be God? But like I said earlier, God says his thoughts are not our thoughts, his ways are not our ways, and his ways are higher. We can't judge God and put Him in a box. What we call order God may think is dysfunction. God's order can be one person laughing, one person crying, one person screaming, one person shaking, one person running etc. Everyone is different and God knows exactly what everyone needs and where they are in their lives. We are finite flesh trying to figure out an infinite God. God knows what He is doing. It's never the manifestations anyways – it's always the fruit in a person's life. Is there a change? Are they in love with God? Look at their lives for fruit. I know I keep saying this over and over and repeating myself because there will be some reading this and be judging it in their heart and thinking, "This is NOT God!" Like I mentioned earlier… how do I know this? Because that is what I have been told. God is not the God of <u>your</u> understanding. Just let Him be God! He's God and you're not!

Travail Begins

Remember my friend whom I talked about earlier from the Brownsville Revival? One evening when I was in prayer, the Holy Spirit came upon me yet again in a way that I had never experienced before. I mean, how many levels are there in God??? How deep and how high? Little did I know… I would soon experience the burden of travail come upon me. Let me just say… there's a difference between someone called to be an intercessor and someone who decides to intercede. Yes, you can decide to intercede on someone's behalf and posture your heart to intercede, and the Holy Spirit will honor you and Heaven will hear your prayer, but when you are called and anointed by the Holy Spirit – you are compelled by an overwhelming urge not of your choosing. God chooses you and then anoints you to stand in the gap – according to grace. It is all Him, not you; you're just the vessel. It's just like someone who is called to the office of the evangelist and someone who evangelizes. The one called has an anointing from the Holy Spirit and there is an extra measure of grace and power that comes upon someone for that ministry.

Intercession from the Holy Spirit is just that – it's from the Spirit as He wills (1 Cor. 12:11); you can't just make it happen. I have never asked for Him to move on me; he just does as He wills. After all; when you pray in tongues, you are praying out the mysteries of God and contending for the faith in the unseen realm. Our intellect could not know the time or the subject of what is being contended for. It is usually only after you answer the call and surrender to the unction that you might be made aware of the subject (and even then, sometimes, you finish laboring in the Spirit and still not know what it is about). Most of those instances are above my need to know. I wish I knew, but I have given up my need to know and just trust Jesus.

1 Cor. 12: 11 "But one and the same Spirit works all these things, distributing to each one individually as He wills." (NKJV)

You can't conjure or hype the groanings and it be genuine; it is the Holy Spirit that comes upon you. None of these moments of intercession did I choose, but rather – the precious Holy Spirit moved upon me. When I experienced travail for the first time, I called my friend from the Brownsville Revival and she didn't even know what to say. I'm not sure she had any experience with travail. Travail in the Spirit is one of the most intense and painful experiences I had ever had up to that point. Oh my God!!!

The definition of travail is: painful or laborious effort. That is exactly what it is. Let me also say again to reiterate, people say God is a gentleman; yes, He is a gentleman when He woos you to become His child, but when you're warring against demons, principalities and powers… it's going to get messy and it's not all nice and sweet. Travail is hard work. Anyway, travail is the most intense, physical manifestation I've ever experienced. It was just as intense as the fire of God that I first experienced. For me, it was a burning sensation in my belly. I was completely overcome. It was so painful that I would (and still do) scream in my pillow, and flip-flop on my bed in agony. My experience with travail is this – it is just as painful as childbirth yet more intense. You feel like you are battling Hell to give birth to something in the Spirit. I felt like I was pushing in the Spirit. It is like the pains of childbirth and it definitely feels like you are birthing something (but in the

Spirit). Below are a couple scriptures about travail in the Bible.

---✦---

Isaiah 66:7-8
"Before she travailed, she brought forth; before her pain came, she was delivered of a man child. [8] Who hath heard such a thing? who hath seen such things? Shall the earth be made to bring forth in one day? or shall a nation be born at once? for as soon as Zion travailed, she brought forth her children." (KJV)

---✦---

Micah 4:9-10
"Now why do you cry aloud? Is there no king in your midst? Has your counselor perished? For pangs have seized you like a woman in labor. [10] Be in pain, and labor to bring forth, O daughter of Zion, Like a woman in birth pangs. For now you shall go forth from the city, You shall dwell in the field, And to Babylon you shall go. There you shall be delivered; There the LORD will redeem you From the hand of your enemies." (NKJV)

---✦---

I knew something was happening in the Spirit that was very intense. The best visual example that I could give to help someone understand (that also helped me understand what happens during travail) was in a book I read from Gwen Shaw of the Endtime Handmaidens.

She said she was suffering physically and was sick, and one of her prayer partners was praying for her and had a vision… and what she saw were the hands of the enemy with black gloves around her neck – gripping and choking her. As the saints were praying for her, she saw the prayers were reaching her, but they were becoming like little red darts and bouncing off the hands of the enemy and they had no effect. It's like the prayers would reach her and hit the hands, but flick right off (her prayer partner said), but when the prayer of travail came up on her… she was given a sword and then she cut the hands of the enemy off. Glory!

That is so powerful; you can just see it? Nothing is done… but first in the Spirit. The Lord has used me many, many times in travail and it is very, very intense, yet I have gotten stronger in the Spirit and am more able to bear up under this strong anointing (or unction) of the Lord when he uses me. I can always tell when travail is coming upon me. I get very agitated and very restless in my own skin and so miserable that I am completely beside myself. This overwhelming sensation (and sometimes a darkness like depression as well) will overshadow me. Even still to this day, in the times leading up to travail, I can't function in normal day to day activities because my spirit man is gearing up for a hellacious battle. But let me say: after these intense times of travail, I am always so very honored and humbled that God would use me for the work of His Kingdom.

The other thing the Lord has always done with me is after I have been in heavy intercession or travail, He always comes and ministers to me with his sweet refreshing presence; it is the most wonderful thing. Oftentimes, the very most intense part of travail doesn't last more than five or ten minutes, but I have to say… it's an incredibly intense and painful five to ten minutes. I think about 15 minutes was the longest. If it was any longer I don't think the body could withstand it. Can I please say this? Your body is the temple of the Holy Spirit. We need to take care of our physical body and I am very healthy, but I could not imagine someone in poor health being used for travail. It takes a toll on me and (because of my experience) I believe it would be hard for someone in poor health to be used for this extreme type of intense prayer. This is the God of the universe we are talking about here… who is touching our mere mortal frail flesh. I have offered my body as a living sacrifice (Rom. 12:2) for the Lord's use. I am truly not my own (1 Cor. 6:19). He has interrupted my daily life many, many times and called me to battle in the Spirit. The timing of the

Spirit and what's going on in the unseen realm is not in sync with humanity's schedule it can be very inconvenient to the flesh. However, God knows your schedule and what you have going on. He knows you have responsibilities and various needs to take care of. I always have time to do what I need to do; He makes sure of it.

✦

I Cor. 6:19 "What? know ye not that your body is the temple of the Holy Ghost which is in you, which ye have of God, and ye are not your own?" (KJV)

✦

There are many more types of prayer as well. I experienced another type described by prayer warriors as: "silent sobbing." There are many times when I just sit and do not say anything because even words cannot adequately describe how I'm feeling. This can happen even while I'm worshiping. An agony of soul will come upon me. I will be in a state of prayer with sorrowfulness of soul that can last for days and even weeks.

Another type of prayer is worship (remember: prayer is communicating with God in the Spirit realm).

Some of the deepest times of worship – are just

sitting and being silent. God is holier than holy and more awesome then awesome, and no human words can adequately describe his magnificent beauty. Maybe you've done what I have done; I'll play "one anointed song" (you know, the one that you have listened to on other occasions) and it took you right into the Spirit? But sometimes I've gotten frustrated because nothing works even after I've tried all those anointed songs, so I would just turn them all off because they were not expressing how I was feeling toward the Lord. Then there are moments in your communication with the Father that are beyond words. Many times I've just sat and closed my eyes and shook my head because the awesomeness of God *is so awesome*… and I am overcome. In these moments, the deep in me is crying out to the deep in God. I love this scripture in Psalms:

Psalms 42:7 "Deep calls to deep, in the roar of your waterfalls; all your waves and breakers, have swept over me." (NIV)

Weeping in Prayer

Another type of intercessory prayer happened to me during church service; I was sobbing uncontrollably and I could hardly stand it. This was, yet again, another new experience for me. This intercession came on me with intense crying and sobbing. I had learned enough by now and knew I needed to go to the back of the sanctuary. The prayer room was locked and I needed to find a place. I remember my mother-in-law telling she would have to get in her car that was parked in her basement garage when she felt intercession coming on. Oftentimes for her, it was early in the mornings when the rest of the family was sleeping, so she did this and didn't disturb anyone. When this happened on Sundays, I would take a cue from her and go to my car to intercede and pray so as not to disrupt the service when I felt intercession coming on me. One time, though, I went to the ladies restroom; that was a mistake, and I only did it once because there were way too many people there for such a private occasion. I was sobbing in the stall in a way that is hard to catch your breath. The wife of one of the assistant pastors' came up to me and said, "Just calm down, just get control of yourself, just calm down." But bless her heart… she just didn't understand. This event I'm describing happened early on and I was unsure what was happening to me. I couldn't even tell her because I was crying so uncontrollably, but after that experience, I just started going out to my car to pray.

Hannah cried out before the Lord it was an unintelligible prayer mixed with sobbing and anguish. God heard her prayers! The scripture doesn't say the Spirit of the Lord came upon her, but her tears got Heavens attention.

✦

1 Samuel 1:10 "And she was in bitterness of soul, and prayed to the LORD and wept in anguish."
(NKJV)

✦

Intercessory Prayer at Church

I love to pray, and now you see – *I had to pray!* And I wanted to get other people to pray, so I approached my pastor and told him that I wanted to have prayer at the church because, as a prayer warrior… I was on fire. So, Gary and I became leaders of intercessory prayer. I couldn't pray enough. I'd go to church before service and pray in the prayer room, but during service they locked the doors… so I had to go outside and get in the car. Lock the prayer room at church? Think about it: the prayer room… locked? Why? I never understood that.

We would meet for intercessory prayer once a

week. Not many people showed up to pray, but that didn't stop me. We would always have a wonderful time when we would gather together and pray. I would love playing the piano in the church sanctuary and worship for hours even if it was just me. There is something great about being all alone in a church that was built to host and worship the King of Kings. A building built with money given from hard working men and women by their blood, sweat and tears – all for the Glory of God and His majesty. I do this now in our church and usually spend about 4-5 hours with Him! It is fun and I love it!!

Let me discuss a little bit about entering into God's presence. Even for me even now, I don't enter right into the Spirit when I'm worshipping or praying. We all have so much going on with our lives and ministry as well. For most people, including myself, it takes me about 15-20 minutes to get "in the Spirit" where my mind is no longer on all the day-to day stresses and drama so I can focus on God. Once you get to that place, however (and sometimes its hard work to get there), it is so glorious. Things that seemed so overwhelming and difficult become small because you get God's perspective and your faith rises up on the inside! There is a chorus in a song that speaks of this place:

"Turn your eyes upon Jesus, look full in His wonderful face, and the things of earth will grow strangely dim, in the light of His glory and grace."

You do have to press-in; our carnal mind can be very resistant, and sometimes (honestly) I have quit and given up. Welcome to fighting the good fight of faith! As they say "at first if you don't succeed try, try again." It is always worth the effort, and you will never be disappointed.

To this day (19 years later… I can hardly believe it has been 19 years since this started), I am extremely sensitive to the presence of the Lord. I will avoid most altar calls and prayer lines because I know what will happen: I will fall out and become spectacle (and I don't want to be). I have been in prayer lines where I was so sensitive and sensed the presence of God that I was thrust backwards by His power into a bunch of chairs scattering them. This really freaks people out. I mean, really… I look at manifestations other people are having and I think they're weird even though I've experienced it myself for 19 years. I was at a service with an evangelist named David Hogan. David is known for being used by God for raising people from the dead. I reluctantly went in his prayer line and got literally airborne and went into the chairs (scattering them once again). The evangelist came up to me afterward and said, "Man, I wish God would move on me like that." I'm thinking… what? I said, "I wish God would use me like you to raise people from the dead."

I really don't know why this happens. I have to say

this again: it is not about the manifestation! It is about a heart change (which I did have). I became radically in love with my Lord and Savior and I couldn't get enough of Him. If God can part the Red Sea, cause Elijah to outrun a chariot, make an axe head float on water, make dead bones live, and so on, then He can do whatever He wants… however He wants… and with whomever He wills… anytime He wills! Sadly, most people won't surrender or yield.

The Glory Pool

I remember one time a few years ago when I was at a service with a young preacher; he was filled with the Holy Ghost and was moving in signs and wonders, and then he said: "There's a 'glory pool' over on the right side of the alter" and, in my mind I'm thinking, "Yeah right... a glory pool; I've never heard that one before. Glory pool – no Way!" Anyway, my girlfriend said:" come on, let's go up there" and I said "no way, I know exactly what's going to happen; I will fall out on the floor and become a spectacle." Well, she finally talked me into it because everybody there was being touched by the Holy Spirit and… he was right! As soon as I walked into the area by the altar, the presence of the Lord was so strong that I fell out in the Spirit and began laughing for almost an hour. It was incredible to say the least. I have part of it on video of me belly laughing with the joy of the Lord. This laughing comes from your belly (it's not in your head). From your belly you feel "rivers of living water" flowing up out of you! That's why you can laugh for over an hour and nothing funny is even being said.

While still on the floor laughing, a lady lying next to me leaned over and told me, "I see the Lord is pulling daggers out of you tonight – of slander, back stabbing and hurtful words" and this experience happened while we were in full-time ministry. The Lord did minister to me while I was laying in His presence and had the joy of the Lord. When I got up from that encounter, my stomach was sore. I didn't laugh the whole hour nonstop, but I would laugh for about 10 to 15 minutes, then get a break, and then laugh again. It was amazing. I believe the Lord was healing me of hurtful things I had experienced up to this point while in full-time ministry. There are a lot of people who need a good laugh in the Holy Spirit who have experienced hurt, pain and depression. God touches and heals people where they are at, but not how you'd think or expect.

Don't judge someone by how they react under the power of the Holy Spirit. You do not know what trauma or pain they have been through, but God does.

✦

Job 8:21 "He will yet fill your mouth with laughing, and your lips with rejoicing." (NKJV)

✦

Psalms 126:2 "Then our mouth was filled with laughter, and our tongue with singing. Then they said among the nations, "The LORD has done great things for them." (NKJV)

✦

Those experiences of refreshing are wonderful because… in the highlight of my personal revival in intercession… there were days when I would be in absolute agony (3-5 days sometimes). There was absolutely no reason for me to even feel this way because there was nothing negative in my personal life or current situation, but now after years of ministry experience, I know this to be the Spirit of God calling me to intercession. In most cases, an intercessor will feel the grief of the Holy Spirit or even be empathetic to the anguish on behalf of the one they are interceding for. Oftentimes for me, it is hard to even speak out loud or voice a prayer, and sometimes it's even difficult to pray in tongues. That is why there is a phrase "sobbing in silence" and this phrase has brought me comfort. The Bible refers to intercession like pregnancy. When a woman is pregnant, she is tired, she is exhausted, she is worn out, and sometimes all she can do is just bear up under the pregnancy because – life and change is happening inside her. This is how intercession is for me. Sometimes I'm carrying a burden inside my spirit, and most of the time I do not know what I'm birthing, but I know it is being born of the Spirit. This is not the same as being compelled to fast and pray for something that is dear to your heart such as health issues or an unsaved loved one which you can and should do, but this is not that. This is carrying a burden from the unseen Spirit realm and bringing it to mankind's reality. I believe I said this before, but it bears repeating. Often times as an intercessor, you are just being used as a conduit and you may not have the need to know. Like a currier carrying classified information in wartime between generals, your job is just to get it through. This would frustrate my husband; he would ask me, "What are you praying about?" and often times… I don't know what's going on. He would tell me just pray in tongues, but that is like coaching a woman who is the middle of contractions and she is in agony, and all she can do is just endure what is happening to her at that moment. I couldn't pray in tongues; I could hardly do anything. When I get to Heaven I want God to show me what was going on during all those times of travail and intercession.

One time, for three days… I was fit to be tied;

miserable; I asked my friend from Brownsville to pray with me and she sensed that it had something to do with the Middle East. At the end of three days, I was praying and then I heard the word "breakthrough." Ironically, on this particular day, I got up from my time of prayer and turned on the TV. The first word I heard was: "There's been a breakthrough! Osama bin Laden has been killed." Could I have been interceding for this historical moment? Seems that way. Woah! That was amazing.

There have been many, many instances where I have just been miserable bearing up under intercession for many days. During this time, I can function, but it is hard. The hardest part is yet to come; like in childbirth, you have to do some of the hardest pushing towards the end. This is when you move from intercession to travail. This does not last as long, but it's the most difficult of all prayers. Travail or heavy intercession will remain until there is a breakthrough at which time I will get a release in my spirit. I wish the Lord would tell me more about what I'm praying for. I'm sure when I get to Heaven I will see and understand. I'm definitely going to ask the Lord about it. Like already mentioned, I really want God to show me what was going on in all those times of travail and intercession.

 I believe during many times of intercession that I

was praying for a myriad of difficulties that we were going to face in our ministry. Our ministry "Regenesis" is a frontline ministry that works with men and women in crisis and in the bondage of addiction. They are hells trophies. We fight in the battle of light against darkness to deliver them from death and destruction.

"God doesn't have many friends, he's searching out those who want to be with Him"

-Tracey McReynolds

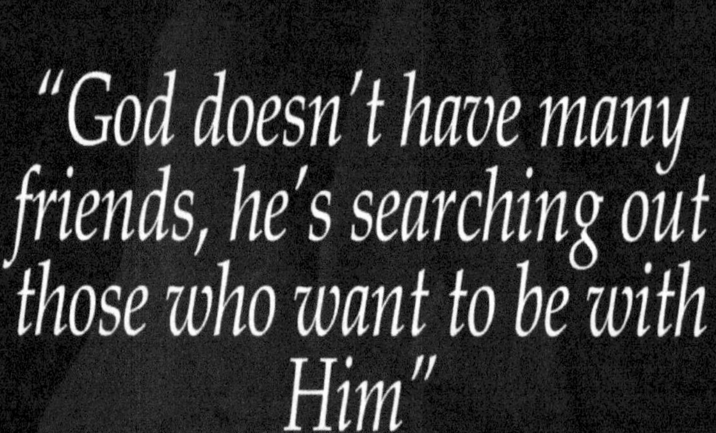

Chapter 6
More Encounters

It seems there are not many people with the same experiences as me. I have read about people having similar experiences, but I would love to meet some (in the flesh) so we could compare notes and encourage one another. I have never seen an angel, although others have, but I have sensed angelic presence. I do believe in "signs that make you wonder" and, therefore, do not believe you should put God in a box. I have served Him long enough to know that He makes my doubting look foolish; and just when you think you have God figured out, he throws a curve ball you never would have expected. He makes things happen in ways I could have never imagined.

✦

1 Cor. 2:9 "Eye has not seen, nor ear heard, nor have entered into the heart of man the things which God has prepared for those who love Him." (NKJV)

✦

Dreams

I have had some amazing dreams. One in particular is etched in my mind. During the peak of my personal revival, I had a dream in which I was told that someone wanted to marry me; that bothered me because I was already married to Gary, and I felt a certain awkwardness in the dream. This man came to me as a Captain; he was dressed in a white suit, and was standing in a hallway of a very large house. The hallway had gold carpet, and posted on the wall were all kinds of awards he had received. I knew in the dream he was a very important person; an honorable and respected man. I saw him, he had dark hair, medium build and not very tall. He told me to pick out my wedding gown, decorations and banquet dishes. So, I went into this huge room where there was everything you could imagine for a wedding; there were beautiful things in that room: dishes, flowers, ribbons etc. In the dream I told him I was already married; He didn't seem to care; He said He was going to marry me. It was an amazing dream. Of course, I knew exactly what it meant and who it was that wanted to marry me. Jesus! I was to become the Bride of Christ.

During the height of my revival, many of the dreams I had were so vivid and real. The flying dreams, in particular, were very real. I can still "see" them in my mind. I've had some amazing flying dreams where I was flying so fast over treetops, flying over cities, in total control, flying like superwoman, with wind in my face, completely overjoyed. Stopping and starting. Those dreams were amazing. One of the most memorable dreams I had was when I was dancing and spinning in an octagon shape ball room with wooden floors and glass all around. The ballroom had a tower of glass that was about 15' tall and I was up in the top of this tower of glass in the air dancing before the Lord. It was glorious. I sensed His strong presence in that dream. It was so real to me.

Night Time Intercession

To this day almost 19 years later, the Holy Spirit still wakes me up just about every night (I'd say at least 5-6 times a week minimum) with shaking and groaning; lots of times I'm in agony and honestly sometimes… I just don't like it. I can't remember the last time I slept through the night, but I know there is something going on that demands intercession happens.

Even after all these years of experiences with intercession, there are times when I will still experience something new for the first time. A few years ago, there were times that I would be awake for three to four hours in utter agony. I would feel it in my knee or elbows – or sometimes both – and there was this intense pressure like pain in my joints. Because this was a new experience, I would rebuke the enemy and plead the blood of Jesus and pray in tongues, but it would not go away… and sometimes it would last as long as four hours and then lift. I was definitely wrestling in the Spirit. I am very eager to find out what was happening during these times of prayer.

I have asked the Lord numerous times what's going on, and then I remember that we run a frontline ministry with a lot of demons, strongholds and addictions… not to mention all of the horrific things going on in the world today. I, amazingly, have never felt tired for work the next day. Like I said earlier, it is so important to take care of your physical body. It is like burden-bearing and heavy lifting.   I also believe it is prophetic, as praying out the mysteries and breakthroughs of things about to happen in the near future – from the spiritual realm into the physical realm.

 I always know when it's time to get in the secret place because I'll feel this annoyance or intenseness in my knees and/or elbows; it's the craziest thing, but it's my queue that it's time to pray and intercede. Honestly, sometimes I just wish I could be left alone. Carrying around burdens and feeling "off" most of the time can be exhausting. Intercession is "intimate" because of the intimacy or sometimes weirdness of how it can look due to the manifestations or prophetic gestures in prayer. Thus, you tend to be alone, want to be alone and have to be alone because it's hard to function with this burden on you. You don't want to be out in public during intercession… just like giving birth is an intimate moment (and not a public moment). But – if God ever lifted this mantle, His presence or this anointing from me – I would be devastated.

I know that sometimes there is too much familiarity with the Lord and I don't want to take Him for granted. It's crazy, but I'm human just like everyone else and the flesh is weak.

Feeling the Heart of God

I have been in many worship services where the presence of the Lord was so strong in our midst. Sometimes I think leadership forgets that they are to host the presence of the Lord, allow Him to move and that they are His servants. During moments where his presence comes in, I know that it is His desire to touch, heal and deliver his people, and the atmosphere is ripe for miracles. I recall one such service when this happened in my church. The atmosphere was thick with the presence of the Lord and the Holy Spirit was grieved because He was not acknowledged nor honored in this moment. His presence actually was cut off and I was shocked and beside myself. During this moment of my revival, you have to understand, I was so close to the Lord and so, so sensitive to his presence. Anyway, the Lord allowed me to feel the pain of His heart and how He was pushed away, dishonored and I was in complete utter agony. He basically let me feel how He feels when He is rejected by His people. I was so broken in this moment. I went into the bathroom inside the prayer room (which was before they locked it) and sobbed uncontrollably. I didn't want to have anyone walk in on me; it was an intimate moment with Jesus. This moment of feeling the heart of God was so overwhelming; I was so overcome, and then, just like the first time I experienced the fire of God, but this time I had to tell the Lord to "turn it off"! I said, "please turn it off… I can't bear up under this pain… it's too much for me" I needed him to lift His pain off me - it was way too much for me to handle.

✦

2 Chronicles 16:9 "For the eyes of the LORD run to and fro throughout the whole earth, to show Himself strong on behalf of those whose heart is loyal to Him." (NKJV)

✦

There have definitely been some monumental times etched in my heart. Another such time was when I felt much grief over lost souls. It was a very heart wrenching, gripping pain that the Lord allowed me to feel. When God lets you feel some of the pain that is in His heart for lost, broken and hurting souls… it's unbearable. God is Love. He has feelings. He wishes that none should parish. The Bible says do not grieve the Holy Spirit. We can wound Him and hurt Him.

✦

Ephesians 4:30 "And do not grieve the Holy Spirit of God, by whom you were sealed for the day of redemption." (NKJV)

✦

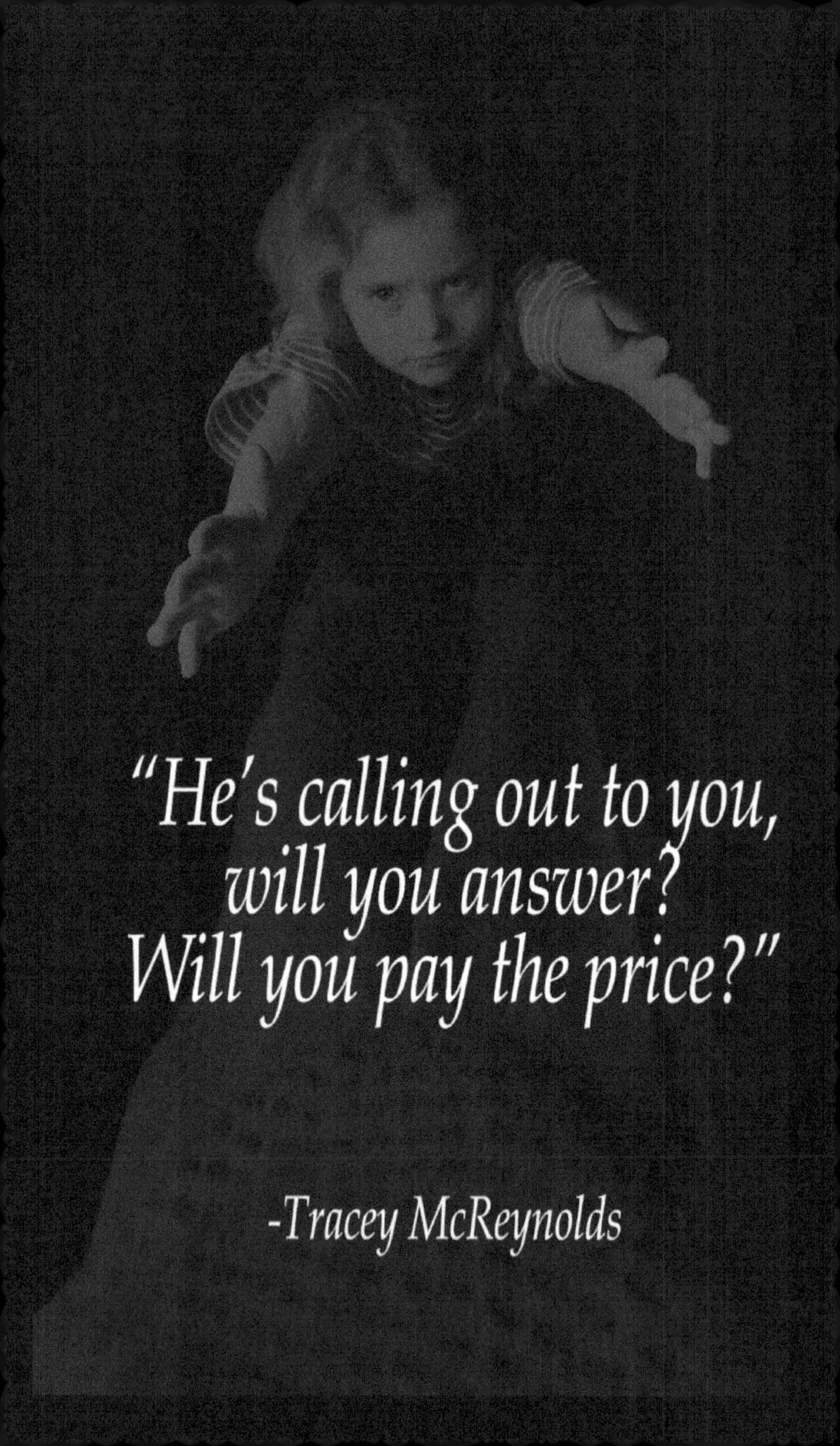

"He's calling out to you,
will you answer?
Will you pay the price?"

-Tracey McReynolds

Chapter 7
Present Day

The past few years have been a different growing season for me. Prior to my personal revival and intercession, God taught me a lot about radical obedience. Now, to this day, God still asks me for acts of obedience and I'm quicker to obey than I was years ago. I am still lover of God. I still love to worship and I still love to be in his presence, but I'm not as lovesick. Just like when you first get married, you're love sick for your mate, but then after you've been married for a few years… that "love-sick" feeling wears off (but you're still committed and in relationship). That season of my revival changed me forever and I'll never be the same. Never!

I'm in a new season now and God is dealing with the intent and motives of my heart, such as my attitude and response toward Him even in difficult times. He is 'growing me up' some more. My revival started in 2002 and then we started Regenesis in 2008. I have grown a lot since we started this ministry, but I know for a fact – I would not be where I am today if I had not experienced this revival that began in 2002. This is a different season, and God is dealing with my attitudes, motives, complaining, comparison, unforgiveness, disobedience, etc.

The last couple years were very difficult for us at the ministry, and one thing I learned is what the Apostle Paul said in Philippians 4:11… to be content in all things and in every circumstance.

Philippians 4:11 "Not that I speak in regard to need, for I have learned in whatever state I am, to be content." (NKJV)

I've really learned that God doesn't care about my need, per se; He cares more about my heart response and my attitude towards Him, my trust in Him, my believing in Him and putting my faith in Him. I've had some very difficult times when I had a really bad attitude towards the Lord which I had to get in check.
I also want to mention my wonderful husband during my revival was – and is now – very supportive of me. He saw the change in me. He has known me for 32 years. I can't imagine what it was like for him to walk in on me while I was in intercession or travail in

our bedroom crying, yelling, shaking, screaming and whatever else I was doing. He knew it was (and is) a sovereign move of God. Even though He has never had the encounters that I have had, he believes in them and knows it is of the Holy Spirit. He completely accepts it and acknowledges what they are… and how the Holy Spirit is working in my life. Gary is a true lover of God.

I could share so much more about present day and what God has done, other tests I've gone through and miracles He has done in my life to this point, **but the main reason for this book is to share my personal revival** and what God did and is still doing and how it is available to whosoever. He is calling out to you; will you answer? Will you pay the price? Will you surrender your plan, purpose, dreams and will for His plan for your life? The scripture in Psalms 37:4 says:

--- ✦ ---

Psalms 37:4 "Delight yourself also in the LORD, And He shall give you the desires of your heart." (NKJV)

--- ✦ ---

One great desire I have is for the fire of God to fall when I lead worship. That is a prayer I'm asking for.

Many people miss the part: "Delight yourself in the Lord". When you delight yourself in the Lord and your desires become His desires, then He is going to answer your desire because they have now become His. Seek first His kingdom and all these things will be added unto you. He already knows the carnal things you have need of, so don't seek things; Seek Him, and Seek His Kingdom.

I am still growing, like all of us, and I have definitely not arrived, but I will choose to keep pursuing Him and seeking the Kingdom to work out my own salvation. The Bible says:

Philippians 2:12 "Wherefore, my beloved, as ye have always obeyed, not as in my presence only, but now much more in my absence, work out your own salvation with fear and trembling*." (NKJV)*

Romans 14:12 "We will all stand before Jesus and give an account of our lives." (NKJV)

May He say unto me… "Well done, My good and faithful servant."

✦

Matt 25:21. "His lord said to him, 'Well done, good and faithful servant; you were faithful over a few things, I will make you ruler over many things. Enter into the joy of your lord.'" (NKJV)

✦

The first step in a relationship with God is through Jesus Christ. If you have not made Jesus the Lord of your life or if you are a believer and you have fallen away, now is the time – today is the day – to come home to the Father! The Bible says:

✦

2 Cor. 6:2… "For He says: "In an acceptable time I have heard you, and in the day of salvation I have helped you." Behold, now is the accepted time; behold, now is the day of salvation." (NKJV)

✦

It is never too late for the prodigal to come back home to the Father. His arms are always open waiting for you to come home.

Please pray this prayer:

Father God I come to you in Jesus mighty name, and I ask for you to forgive me of all my sins; I believe that you died on the cross for me for the remission of my sins; I want you to be the Lord and Savior of my life, and I want to be in fellowship with you and follow you all the days of my life. Father, this day, I also ask that you would baptize me in the Holy Spirit and Fire. Amen!!

He is your satisfaction, your peace, your hope, your dreams, and your everything!

Pursue Him always, you will never be disappointed. He is a Good, Good Daddy God!!

Prayer: Father God, In Jesus name, I ask that You encounter my friend reading this book. That You would give them a supernatural hunger and thirst for You. That as they seek You with their whole heart – they would find You. That You would show Yourself strong in their life. I ask that they would have supernatural dreams and visions. I ask that You fill them with a fresh touch from Heaven NOW! In the mighty name of Jesus. Come, Holy Spirit Come! We love you, God!

If this book touched your heart and you would like to share a testimony or comment, Please email me at:

whattheheckisprayeranyway@gmail.com

facebook.com/whattheheckisprayeranyway

P.O. Box 151
Sutherland, Virginia 23885

TRACEY MCREYNOLDS has been married over 35 years to Gary, her best friend, lover and partner in Ministry. She proudly served in the U.S. Army for 5 ½ years and earned solider of the year honors. In 2008, she and her husband started "Regenesis" a frontline outreach ministry with a focus of residential recovery programs for men and women. In 2019, they founded Spirit Life Worship Center Church where Gary is Senior Pastor. Tracey is an anointed prayer and worship leader and loves being in the presence of the Holy Spirit. She desires for others to experience the presence of the Holy Spirit and to have an encounter with God that radically impact their life.